THE V
OF
HEALER

Peter Gill

Introduction
by
Lilla Bek

THE MERCIER PRESS

The Mercier Press, 4 Bridge Street, Cork
24 Lower Abbey Street, Dublin 1

ACKNOWLEDGEMENTS

*It is with great pleasure that I dedicate this book to Joa Bolendas in
gratitude for her help and guidance on many occasions.*

*In addition I would like to thank Lela Fischli for kindly editing my
manuscript and bringing it all together and my good friend John Hill for
his ready counsel and encouragement. I am also indebted to Margaret
Redmond who typed the manuscript from my handwritten notes.*

And my thanks also go to Elizabeth for her help and encouragement.

Printed in Ireland by Colour Books Ltd.

CONTENTS

ETERNITY

As the stars are numberless in their beauty
And Space infinite in its compassion
As Time is unlimited with its Grace
So have we been granted the Blessing of Love
That we might enjoy the Wonders of Creation
As we share these gifts in our Journey through Eternity
To become the companions of God and each other for ever.

INTRODUCTION

LILLA BEK

Peter Gill is what I would call a full time healer. I do not mean to say that Peter works a 36 hour week, five days a week, with a compulsory lunch break from 1 pm to 2 pm each day. When a person has seriously devoted himself or herself to an art such as healing for many years, as Peter has done, then there comes a subtle moment in time when one's every movement, every thought, and every action is inspired by a motive to heal. This is what I mean when I say Peter Gill is what I would call a full-time healer.

The Way of a Healer is a self-portrait. From the hands of a healer, to the heartbeat of the planet, it wanders through and explores the practices and philosophies that motivate and inspire a healer. Peter's book is not only a tapestry of life, but a tapestry of healing, and a rich tapestry at that.

Peter introduces us to the life of a healer. He encourages us to see, hear, touch, speak and live as a healer does. He provides us with an intimate glimpse into the private life of a healer. The mind of a healer, the heart of a healer and the motivations of a healer are all unveiled.

Turn to any page in this book, pick any paragraph, and there before you is a rich and profound contemplation. Peter's style of writing is like his style of healing, warm, friendly, accurate and to the point. No word is wasted; every word is helpful. Peter's style of writing is also very access- ible. He has taken great care to clarify and make clear that which he writes about.

One of the strengths of *The Way of a Healer* is that Peter imparts many of the personal experiences he has had along his healing journey. Peter's experience as a healer makes him exceptionally well qualified to write this book. As a healer unfolds the precognitive visions, instant inner promptings, intuitive knowings, the memory of a past life, all these strange events become a part of one's experience.

As well as being an exponent of healing, Peter has also been instrumental in pioneering and publicising the art of healing in Ireland. Together with his wife, Elizabeth, he has organised and networked numerous healing events over the years. It was through this work that Peter, Elizabeth and myself first came into contact some ten years ago now. Since that time, it has been one of the blessings in my life to return to Ireland again and again to see and work with Peter and Elizabeth.

If one had to identify a single strength and attribute of Peter's work, I would have to plump simply for this: *his example*. An essential, though very subtle, aspect of the way of a healer is the example they, often unconsciously, set for others. Peter has been a help and inspiration to many, many people up until now. With the success of *The Way of a Healer*, you may find that Peter helps and inspires you also.

LILLA BEK
SUNBURY ON THAMES

1

GLIMPSES OF THE
INVISIBLE REALMS

I remember clearly one sunny September day when I was eleven years old sitting down under a tree, and thinking. At that time I knew what I wanted to do when I grew up and that was to race motor-cars. From a very early age I had been fascinated by them and my father had taught me by progressive stages from sitting on his knees and holding the steering wheel until, with sufficient cushions behind my back, I could just reach the pedals and manage on my own. I realised, as I sat there and contemplated my ambitions, that nobody was just going to come along and present me with a racing car and the means to run it. If that was what I really wanted I would have to do something about it myself and make a beginning and put a plan into action there and then. It occurred to me that a motor-cycle would be a much more feasible proposition and a project more likely of attainment and it would be a stepping stone to greater things. I also knew that at some stage I must study religion for I had a deep inner feeling, or urge, to discover and understand the reason for our being in this world and where we came from and where we went to, and, indeed, our relation to the stars themselves. So, in a simple, clear-cut fashion, I mapped my life out ahead of me; I would race motor-cycles and cars for as long as possible, and maybe have some involvement with aeroplanes and then — when I was sixty I would study religion!

I determined there and then to make a start and decided I would save every penny I could and no longer spend my pocket money on sweets and other such things — but just go on saving. And so I got on my bicycle and pedalled off into the local village newsagent's shop and enquired if there were any magazines on motor-cycles. Being told that there was a weekly one I then asked my father could I change my weekly boys' magazine to the motor-cycle one — and so, my education into the world of wheels began. After a while, my father, who gave me every encouragement, said he would add £1 to every £1 that I saved although that was quite a financial strain for him. And so it was that at sixteen I got my first motor-cycle, one far beyond my earliest expectations, and rode in my first race the following year when I was seventeen.

I studied engineering and upon qualifying joined the Royal Air Force as the Second World War had already started. After four years in the RAF, like so many other young people at that time whose careers had been interrupted by the war, it was not so easy to pick up the threads again after demobilisation. I started racing again but had a very bad accident which I was most fortunate to survive. It was raining heavily at the time and I came off on a very fast bend at about 80 mph and hit a telegraph pole. My injuries were extensive and many times since I have been told by practitioners, when having a massage or other treatment, that it was a miracle I survived. I did race once again afterwards and then, one evening, received a telephone call from a friend in England who asked me to ride his machines the next year. That would have been an ideal arrangement, but something inside me made me turn down the offer. It seemed that there was no real reason why I should still be alive and little point in being saved just to continue on the same path. I felt that there must be something more in life to do and, in a way, this was a turning point that affected the future course of events.

From time to time after the accident I did not feel well and one day, not long after we were married, I became ill. My wife, Elizabeth, who was a wonderful nurse, helped me regain my health. One day while I was lying in bed she gave me a copy of the Bible and said 'you are always saying you have no time to read — you've no excuse now!' And so my study of religion was brought forward in time from my planned programme of so long ago. At that time she also gave me a copy of *There is a River* which was the story of the life of Edgar Cayce — America's best documented psychic. It instantly struck a chord within me, especially the philosophy of life that he expressed. There was no difficulty in accepting it because it seemed to find an immediate recognition from deep within.

This was the beginning of our esoteric studies. We decided to set aside one night per week for study, and this we did together for many years on our own as we knew no one else at that time with whom we could discuss these matters. We did a postal study course of Rosicrucian monographs because there was no lodge or group in Ireland at that time, and it was the only source of information available to us. It proved invaluable as the years unfolded.

Some years later we got a request from Hugh Lynn Cayce, Edgar Cayce's son, whom we had never met, asking if we could arrange a public lecture as they were sending a lecturer to Europe for the first time. And so began our work of presenting to the public, through different speakers, the ancient wisdom and knowledge contained within esoteric teachings. In those early days of the 1960s this was not easy as there was a great deal of scepticism among people generally, and from within the church particularly, which sometimes was openly opposed to such ideas. It is interesting that when we went to put an advertisement in the papers for our first public lecture, one of the national newspapers refused to take our advertisement because the title of the lecture contained the word *Psychic!*

Partly because of this, and also because we felt that it was important to do something and put into practice many of the things we believed in, we started, with one or two other people, a small group who met regularly on Wednesday evenings for a period of prayer and meditation for absent healing for those who were ill or in hospital. We felt that working in this way would not be against anyone's ideology or religious beliefs, and it would also give people an opportunity to participate and contribute in some way to the work. Sometimes there would only be two or three people but the intention was that there should always be at least two people meeting at 9 pm every Wednesday evening for this purpose — this often gave people in hospital a great deal of comfort and a sense of presence and being remembered. We called the group the 'Circle of Light' and, it has, naturally over the years expanded in size and also in number — with meetings continuing regularly ever since. Also at this time we started the beginnings of a small library which has now grown into a large lending library and book service. Books often were, and still can be, a marvellous way of starting people on a voyage of discovery which can affect their lives deeply.

My first close encounter with healing occurred when a friend, Doris, who ran a healing prayer group, rang one day to say that she had a friend from Wales staying with her who was a very good healer. She had kindly offered to give me a treatment as, at that time, there was a small growth on my leg which had become troublesome. I had just seen a specialist who had said he would cut it out but, as he was about to go on holiday, an appointment was made for three or four weeks hence. When I went to Mary for my healing session my leg was quite inflamed and irritable. To my surprise she put her hands not only on the affected part of my leg, but also over different parts of my body and head. Over the next few days my leg improved considerably but the growth was still there. The time to see the specialist came and I went for my appointment and told him that I had received healing whilst he had been away and wished to postpone his operation. He was insistent that if it hadn't gone within two weeks he would have to operate, and agreed to wait but said he didn't believe it would go. Not long afterwards it just fell off one day, leaving no scar. Another side effect was that at that time I was also experiencing very severe night sweats so that I would frequently have to get up and change my night clothes. They stopped entirely after that treatment and this was my first experience of energies being brought back into balance — something of which I was unaware at that time.

As the years unfolded we were fortunate to become friends with a number of remarkable people who greatly influenced our thinking and confirmed many inner thoughts and beliefs. It is sometimes difficult to separate or highlight where a certain idea came from, it is as though it was always just there and yet one day someone declares or speaks it for the first time.

Our contact with Ronald Beesley, the founder of White Lodge and the College of Psycho-Therapeutics in Kent, England, brought us in touch with the courses he ran on healing and the techniques that he taught on how to use the hands to balance the various energies and energy points of the body. His courses of instruction became, in time, the foundation of our own work and our direct involvement in the world of healing. His ability to read the Aura and diagnose from it was remarkable. Time and time again at public lectures or on courses he would demonstrate in very real terms the fact that the pattern and colour of the different energy fields surrounding the body are a living history and carry the indelible imprint of every event and illness in our lives – even the indication of an illness which has not yet manifested at a physical level. His extraordinary gifts at all levels of extrasensory perception opened up for us an awareness of the tremendous untapped talents which lie dormant in all human beings, for the most part unused. By profession an engineer, he was an exceptional healer and all in all he was, truly, a practical mystic.

Another of these exceptional people whom we were fortunate to meet and learn from is Flower A. Newhouse, a gifted mystic and the founder of the Christward Ministry and Questhaven retreat in California. Her mission was to bring back to the world the reality of angels, the Angel

Kingdom and the truth of mystery teachings. Her perception of the angelic realm, the kingdom of those luminous beings, believed in by so few, yet mentioned so frequently in religious writings and 295 times in the christian bible alone, is extraordinary. On our first visit we were naturally fascinated to hear of her insights into this 'other world'. As we were walking one day, on that first visit, I asked her, 'Flower — how do you see the angels?'

She stopped and replied, 'Oh, Peter, I see them just as clearly as I see you standing there!'

To go for walks with her along nature trails was an experience never to be forgotten as she described for us the wonders of a world hidden from our eyes but so obviously clearly visible to her. On one walk up a mountain trail with her we stopped at the foot of a large pine tree, with a beautiful view all around. Flower told us that this was the place of a King Deva. A Deva is that branch of the Angel Kingdom that watches over and cares for and ministers to all the growing things of the forest. During the day the Deva worked and floated through the forest and hillside, blessing and charging all the trees, plants and grasses. The King Deva greeted us and sent us a blessing which Flower interpreted for us as: 'The currents of the forest greet and bless you. You go with strength, courage, power and inspiration.'

Through this actual experience I became aware that there is an intelligence deep within every living cell and organ, in every plant and tree; and that the elements themselves come under the control and direction of high intelligences who form and move the weather patterns. In this context we might remember the gospel story where Jesus stilled the storm and spoke to the wind and to the sea (Mark 4:39, 41):

> And he arose, and rebuked the wind, and said unto the sea, Peace, be still. And they feared exceedingly, and said to one another, what manner of man is this, that even the wind and sea obey him?

One exceedingly hot summer we were in the south of France at the Spiritual Centre of the Fraternité Blanche Universelle, whose great teacher was Maitre Omraam Mikhael Aivanhov. For months there had been no rain and the ground was parched and like tinder. Someone asked him if he would ask for some rain and he replied: 'They have their work to do. But, we will see'. That day we all gathered as usual for the midday meal in the large dining hall which accommodates over a thousand people. All meals are taken in absolute silence in order that one should focus the attention entirely upon the act of eating and also to encourage an awareness of one's actions. In the middle of the meal the Maitre, in a rare exception to the rule, suddenly pointed his finger upwards and spoke just three words. 'They are considering.' Within a few minutes torrential rain pelted down drenching everywhere just like a proverbial cloud burst. Only there were no clouds — just a clear sky. The rain slashed first against one side of the building and then against the other. After a short while it stopped as suddenly as it started. Outside steam was rising from the ground and there were puddles everywhere and little rivulets flowing across the pathways. It was a remarkable demonstration of communication and co-operation between the intelligence of another realm and ours.

Aivanhov constantly stressed the importance of working upon ourselves in order to eliminate our weaknesses so that we might express more perfectly our divine nature. That we should strive to establish everywhere law and order — in the world about us and within ourselves. That we should live in harmony with the forces of nature and the universe. Every year from Easter to Michaelmas he would rise at dawn with his followers to meditate and greet the sunrise. A discipline he maintained until well into his eighties.

With increased awareness, we find that many of our observations are heightened. As an illustration I'd like to describe a small experience which occurred as I drove to work one morning, and which made a deep impression on me.

There was a route that I used to like to take because it was quieter than the main road and there was less traffic. One suburban road in particular was a favourite because it was planted on both sides of its length with beautiful flowering cherry trees. As I turned into the road this particular morning and approached the first tree there was a little flurry as a few petals fell to the ground. I thought how nice it looked, and as I drew near the second, exactly the same thing happened. I thought to myself, 'that's strange, I didn't know there was any wind this morning'. So I looked at the other side of the road and there was no movement. In fact, every tree was perfectly still and motionless. When I came to the third tree again there was the same flurry of a few petals falling like snowflakes and I suddenly realised that 'someone' was greeting me and trying to attract my attention. I quickly returned a mental greeting and at every tree the same thing happened until the end of the road. But only on the side on which I was driving! That morning I went to work with a great feeling of being uplifted.

One might be inclined to ascribe such an occurrence as a coincidence, or even imagination. But when the same kind of thing happens on a number of occasions, then one has to become more aware of what it is that one is observing. At the end of one holiday we had to catch an early morning train and as we walked down the road from where we were staying, there was a rustle in the leaves of the first tree as we came abreast of it. And again the same thing from each tree as we passed in a kind of farewell — *au revoir*.

Another person who has taught me much is Lilla Bek. To be with her is always a most enriching and sometimes exciting experience. Her unique ability to 'see' enables her to look into objects and discern their structures and energies, from the microcosmic level to the macrocosmic. She is able to look into the structures of the atoms and see the shapes and forms of their energies and even hear the beat of their pulse, their hum or note. And she can also look out into the great star systems and galaxies, or back into time and describe events

16

of the past which are indelibly imprinted upon the skein of time and space.

Once when she was staying with us she wanted a pattern for knitting. Elizabeth told her where there was a box full of women's magazines which would probably have something suitable. When Lilla got to the box she was surprised to see, as she told us afterwards, 'a living green energy coming from the box'. As she hunted through the magazines she came across a couple of forlorn but still alive plants which had long ago been forgotten at the bottom of the box!

Lilla is a vice-president of the National Federation of Spiritual Healers and a very good healer and counsellor herself. With her great sensitivity she is able to to tell many things about people and help them to understand their problems, and give them guidance as she sees their path unfolding before her; but always with the deep wisdom not to divulge more than she is allowed to. However, she considers herself to be a researcher and works with doctors and others in trying to raise our awareness and understanding of the world of energies in which we are immersed and of the many energies which are a part of our very make-up.

Being with such people makes one more aware and conscious of the super-sensible worlds. Even if we are not 'psychic', we can learn to see with heightened sensitivity, to be truly more observant. We can listen with keener attention to all the different nuances and tones and hear the sound within the sound. We can raise our sense of smell that will tell us when there are angel presences around, or warn us of negative influences or even of the presence of disease.

In recounting some personal experiences in this way it is because they have had such an important part to play in my life, in helping me to understand better much that I have learned. They have also confirmed for me the reality that we are not just encased in this concrete material world but have very strong links with more subtle dimensions of existence. In paying attention to these experiences they have opened my awareness to the fact that we all have within us our own inner teacher and healer — our Higher Self.

In giving these examples, it is with the hope that they will encourage others to also be guided by their own personal experiences which are very real and alive and can serve as guide-lines along their way of life. Most of us do not have the gift of clairvoyance or clairaudience but we can develop and sharpen our senses and refine them by practice so that they become better instruments for our use. We can raise or heighten our sensitivity or awareness to a higher level so that it becomes for us a sixth sense, for the sixth sense is only one or all of our natural five senses raised to another dimension. We may find as we begin to work in this way that we have a greater facility with one particular sense and we should cultivate its use and rely upon it, but, of course, not neglect the others.

We can expand our vision with practice so that we become more observant in noticing in things and people subtle changes that herald some impending change in circumstances or in health. Just as by noticing the movement and actions of birds and animals we can see that they are aware of some change in weather patterns or that the right time to migrate is close at hand. By closely watching for subtle changes in movements and reactions of people these can tell us of some unease or worry, of some fear or anxiety; or of course the opposite, a change for the better.

Every object carries a vibration and every vibration carries a message. We can train our sense of touch to feel into things and to read the message from an object, or the needs of a person. Blind people with practice can determine one colour from another just by passing their fingertips over them. We can emulate them in this and other ways by concentrating upon and developing our sense of touch. In massage and other body therapies our hands, after a while, will automatically be drawn to the site of pain or to any place of need.

One of my friends who is a well known pianist will,

before any important concert, sit down and practise the particular piece of music many times. But he does not put the music on the music stand in front of him, but a book or the daily newspaper and reads that while his hands are 'learning' the notes! In a sense, his fingers cannot ultimately strike a wrong note. And we have only to watch the feet of a beautiful dancer as they move across the stage or dance floor to be aware that somehow consciousness is in the feet.

That objects do carry vibrations was dramatically dem-onstrated when we were staying with a friend who would 'look' at the morning's post and pick out those letters which shone or scintillated brightly with energies of love and joy; but not being so drawn to those which were dull or dark. On this particular occasion, there was one letter she did not like the feel of and, as it happened to be from a person who had invited her to come and give a lecture, she thought perhaps that they might not want her to come for some reason. So she picked up the telephone and said that if for any reason it was not convenient for them to have her or did not want her to come, then that was quite all right with her. The person replied: 'But of course we want you to come, we're looking forward to it. Whatever made you think we didn't?' And so it turned out during the conversation that this person had had a row with his assistant and after some angry words between them he had fired him. He then immediately sat down and wrote the letter, which was impregnated with all those angry thoughts.

Energies are constantly streaming from our hands, the very essence of our being, to influence everything that we touch. We are surrounded by an atmosphere of our own thoughts and emotions. After this experience I have been unable to put any letter in a letter box without first holding it in my hands for a few moments and concentrating upon the particular quality which I wish it to carry. We must remem-ber that a letter is our ambassador. It is the only link we have with the recipient and the effect that it has upon the person is all important. So even a letter can carry a message other than its contents.

We can use this sense of touch in other ways too. Should we ever purchase a piece of second-hand jewellry we should always hold the item in our hands for a few moments to feel its vibrations, whether they are pleasant or otherwise. For all objects carry influences from the past, from the wearer, and we do not want to take up other peoples' problems. If we have attained a skill in doing this, which is called psychometry, then we could use it to tell us something about a person if they allow us to hold in our hand a ring or watch or something that they have been wearing.

We are embedded in these super-sensible worlds and can react to their impulses and messages. We can go with them and they can protect us or further our well-being. By being connected we can be warned of impending danger to ourselves or others, and sometimes anticipate and stop the onset of some disease or illness. We can become more conscious and co-operate with higher intelligence and in this way become a healer.

One day after lunch I became strongly aware of a beautiful aroma and thought perhaps that it must come from one of the many plants and flowers which abound in every room in our house. So I went around all the plants in the room and smelt them to see if I could identify the perfume, but could find none that matched. All the time there was the thought of a certain friend in England in my mind, whom I seemed to connect with the perfume. As the sensation was very strong I rang that evening to find out how she was and if, perhaps, she had been thinking about me at lunchtime. Yes, she had been talking about me and what I had smelt was 'the sweet aroma of prayer'. So, I was being looked after, for there is none of us who can not do with a little help now and then.

We can benefit greatly by paying attention to our intuition and acting upon it in whatever way it manifests to us, even if we do not fully understand at the time. One evening I had a very strong dream about a business friend and it seemed that he was under a great deal of stress and at a very low ebb both physically and mentally, and that his car had been wrecked, although he was uninjured. Wondering why I had this dream, which did not seem to be connected with me, I decided to phone him. He thanked me and said yes, he had been overdoing things greatly and had been driving long distances until late into the night. He had nearly crashed twice and had realised that he should take things more quietly, but hadn't done so. However, now he would try and re-arrange his affairs and leave himself more space.

Another time I felt impressed to sit down and write a letter to my old headmaster, something I was not in the habit of doing. He was then getting on in years and had retired a long time ago. I told him in the letter how much my time in school had meant to me especially the ideals he had tried to instil of integrity, sportsmanship and fair play in all things, and that scarcely a day passed that I did not somehow think of him. I posted the letter and felt glad. Just a few days later I heard that he had died and I was doubly glad that I had acted on the impulse and had not delayed. Sometime later I met him in sleep on the higher planes and we had a long conversation together. It was granted to me to explain something about the continuity of consciousness and the reality of other dimensions. We parted and I was happy in the knowledge that he would continue with his great work of helping and guiding people and finding new ways to do so. It was not until many years later that someone told me that his family had said that a few days before he died he had received a letter which he read over and over again, but which he would show to no one. When he died they found it by his side. It is not often that we get confirmation of our actions but we must try to follow our intuition and leave the results to take care of themselves. There is an old saying that 'dreams are unopened letters from the soul'. We should pay much more attention to this correspondence because through it we may be given much guidance which will be helpful to us and others. Also, the more we work with them the more expansive they will become and lead us into other dimensions of experience and reality. It has been said that those who are in control of their dreams will be in control of their state of being after death.

When someone constantly comes into our mind and we do not know why and cannot contact them, we should always take it as a signal to pray for them. We should pray that they may be surrounded by the light of Christ and guided by the Holy Spirit. Sometimes we may have had a great day and gone to bed feeling tired but in the best of form only to wake up in the morning feeling down, low and dejected. We wonder 'What is wrong with me that I feel like this?' But it may not be you at all. If, as a healer, we are helping people then sometimes we become the only link in the chain with someone who is desperately in need of help. Instinctively they will think of you strongly, and unconsciously or otherwise you will feel and pick up their thoughts. Of course the low feeling could have something to do with you but, in any event we should take the problem, known or otherwise, up into the light and ask that it be dissolved and resolved and that the person concerned may receive the help they need. Don't just let it hang around and do nothing about it.

There are days, too, when we may feel low because of changing weather patterns or electrical tensions in the atmosphere or because of thunder storms or earthquakes. Even though these may not be directly in our area we can feel their tensions. Some people are very much affected by the moon and others by changes in the sun such as solar flares or sunspot activity. And, of course, we can have our high days when the atmosphere feels light and vibrant. Even the wind has different sounds and temperaments. We must learn to be aware of our own changing moods and the origin of them by strengthening our link with higher intelligences.

We must become consciously aware of this link with the super-sensible worlds, a link that can be cultivated by anyone who so desires and who wholeheartedly apply themselves to develop it. This needs practice, dedication and patience, but this heightened sensitivity is an instrument of every healer which is open to all.

2

HEALING, HEALTH AND WHOLENESS

Health is a subject which is of the greatest concern to everybody but, strangely enough, it is something to which many of us pay little or no attention; that is, until something goes wrong. With the onset of some illness, a pain in the back or some other disorder, the whole of our attention becomes riveted upon the problem. It is difficult for us to take our mind off the malady — even for a moment. It is then that we become truly aware of the wonderful gift and joy of living without conscious effort. In good health we are mostly unconscious of the existence of our body; hour by hour, day by day it goes on doing its work of keeping all the necessary bodily functions — such as, for example, circulation, digestion, respiration — under control and working smoothly without our conscious knowledge or attention. We take so much for granted.

In the very old days in China, the people used to pay their doctor, or physician, as he was called, when they were well but not when they were ill. It was his job to keep them well and fit. The accent was upon health and its maintenance and preservation rather than upon the curing of an irregularity which should not have occurred in the first place: a sort of social health scheme in reverse. A good concept, but one which perhaps would cause a few eyebrows to be raised if proposed today! However, there is a renewed interest in health in general and many people indulge in 'keep-fit' exercises and engage in sports and other outdoor activities with this end in view. This is good but there is a great deal more to health than physical exercise. Diet, too, plays an important part and especially the realisation of the value of natural foods and the proper balance of essential nutrients. All of these, though, are only essential parts of a greater whole, for we must not forget mental and spiritual health and these, unfortunately, are at a very low ebb all over the world today. The frequent outbreaks of violence and destruction to be seen everywhere are evidence of this. There is a waiting list to get into prisons and the mental hospitals are full. It is a paradox that when the churches are empty, the hospitals and prisons are full.

Whilst there is much that we can do to achieve, maintain and preserve good health, all of this can be set at naught through unbalanced thoughts, acts and attitudes of mind. We can gain as much by avoidance, that is by not doing that which is detrimental to our physical, mental and spiritual health, as we can by concentrating only on a part of that which we know to be good. It is so easy to forget the bad. As in all things we have to strike a balance by working steadily in a positive manner whilst at the same time gradually eliminating the negative aspects. That is, if we constantly concentrate upon our weaknesses and faults our thinking can never rise above them. In a sense, we hold ourselves back by always focusing our attention upon them. It would help if we raised our sights a little and strove to achieve some higher goal or ideal. In this way, our faults would gradually fall behind as we endeavour to achieve a higher level of being.

Once health has broken down and illness has manifested at a physical level, then all the body's natural healing forces are marshalled to bring about a return to a normal state of health. When this has been achieved, it is said that the condition has been 'cured'. A cure, by whatever means, is a healing, but the quality of the healing depends upon many factors and goes deeper than just the external symptoms.

When we speak of healing, we are referring to health: health as wholeness. That word, 'wholeness', implies a number of separate parts coming together to comprise a complete whole. We are accustomed to the concept of body, mind and soul, and health is the harmony of these three, functioning and acting together in co-ordination and co-operation, three in one. Should, however, these three aspects of a person not function together harmoniously, we have dis-harmony or dis-ease. If a state of dis-ease is allowed to continue unchecked, it will ultimately manifest in the body as disease or illness. Healing is bringing these separate parts back into balance or harmony again. In general, today's western medical treatment is concerned mainly with effects rather than causes, whilst healing is concerned primarily with causes. When a cause has been found, understood, and eliminated, then healing can take place. Spiritual healing aims to reach and deal with the root of the problem, the origin of the state of disharmony, and not just to concentrate upon the symptoms. Often many of the problems and difficulties in life which are experienced today can be related to some sort of spiritual disturbance or frustration where the soul has been denied the opportunity of finding that expression which it came here to fulfil. The body is often the *victim* and not the *cause* of the problems which, from time to time, afflict it.

The healing to which I refer touches the soul or spiritual aspect of a person, for healing comes from within, and the healer is merely the agent or channel through which divine power may flow to activate the healing process. When the healer, through attunement, invokes a higher dimension — God — or whatever one's understanding is of the ultimate source of all being, then changes may be brought about which are normally considered to be impossible, within the framework of the third dimensional physical laws. In such cases, a healer acts as a link in the chain whereby God, man and cosmos are brought back into balance and harmony with one another, that condition which should be our natural state. However, should a healer, for any reason, not be in a state of spiritual, mental or emotional harmony, then it will be difficult to raise the corresponding level within the patient. A healer should, therefore, always strive to maintain a state of inner harmony and peace and be at one with God, the cosmos and the world at large.

In days long gone by the healer and priest were one and the same person. The two roles were not separated. He was physician, counsellor and teacher. Today it is time for religion to adapt the religion of science into its thinking and teaching, for science to accept the science of religion into its researches and investigations. These disciplines must somehow be merged, and the art of healing can help bring this about. Healing is inherent in both religion and science and, for this reason, its scope cannot be limited. Sometimes healing reaches into the very surroundings of people and their relationships.

One day, a young mother was brought by a friend to see me. Her baby had been born with cerebral palsy and it was naturally a tremendous disappointment and traumatic experience for both parents. Life was difficult in just trying to cope with the situation and it was not made any easier by the fact that they were sharing a house with another couple and relationships were very strained, to say the least. It was important that the house was close to the clinic where the child had to be brought each day.

The mother had never been to a healing session before and was not sure what to expect but was willing to try any possibility. The infant was unable to sit on its own, having to be held and propped up and it moved about continuously. With the infant being held on the mother's knee, I tried to give a treatment, but it was difficult because of the child's restlessness. While I was working, the thought came that really it was the young woman who needed help the most. She was obviously under a great deal of stress in trying to deal with the many demands that were made upon her. So, feeling that there was not a great deal I could do for the child at this stage, I asked her if she would like a treatment.

After a moment's thought, she said, yes, she would. As she sat down, her friend took the child off into another room and immediately it started crying loudly. I could sense that the mother's instant reaction was to get up and run to the child, but she didn't and stayed where she was and relaxed greatly. After the treatment, she stood up and shook herself and said, 'I feel all connected again'. It is surprising how often people use that phrase. After she left, I did not see her again but several months later, met her friend one day by chance and enquired after her. She said, 'Oh, I must tell you. That night after she went home it seemed as though something strange and powerful was taking place within the house, almost frighteningly. Her husband had said that it was as though a tremendous battle was taking place all night long. Then, in the morning, all was still, calm. Just like the quiet after a storm'. From that day, relationships in the household changed completely and there was peace and harmony, and co-operation and friendship grew.

We must never limit the scope of spiritual healing and its outreach. In the above case perhaps the important thing was first of all to get the environment right so that the child could be brought up in helpful and harmonious surroundings.

Another similar case was when someone rang one day to make an appointment. She had been attending another healing organisation, but for one reason or another, felt she would like to make a change. An appointment was arranged and we sent her some information on our work. Some days later, the phone rang and she said that, having got the information, she thought she wouldn't come after all as it seemed that we were working along very similar lines to the people she had been with. I spoke to her and said that, while appreciating her concern, I felt that it was a pity if she didn't do something, as her complaint was fairly serious. I suggested that, as she had already made an appointment, perhaps she would come along and we could have a talk; that maybe I would 'be a stepping stone to someone else who could help her'. In healing, it is so important never to close the door, and always to offer some alternative.

The appointed day came and we met and talked, and at

the end of the session, I asked if she would like a treatment while she was here, without any obligation on her part to accept. She said that she would, and at the end made an appointment to come back again the following week. On the first visit, she had seemed somewhat reserved, which was quite natural, and as though things were weighing heavily upon her. On the second visit, she was much more relaxed but there was no great change in her physical condition. Owing to circumstances, it was not possible to make another appointment for a couple of weeks, and I sometimes wondered if she would turn up. But the day before the due date, she rang up to confirm if the appointment was in order, and I was pleased.

When she came in, she said, 'I don't know if it has anything to do with it but since I came to see you, a lot has happened in my life'. Then she told me that she now felt much happier and that her relationships within the family were much better. Later she was kind enough to write to say how she was getting on and wrote, 'The moral of the story is, perhaps, our prayers are being attended to'.

Others have also said how they have been able to cope much better and look at life with more courage and calmness so the family relationships have improved. In many cases, the question of relationships was never mentioned but this was the level which was touched through the healing session. It was only later that we were told of this aspect of their lives.

It seems sometimes in healing that it is important, first of all, to get the groundwork right: for the house to be put in order, so to speak. And this can be done without any conscious or intentional effort on the part of the healer. Some other dimension is at work and the healer is merely the agent or catalyst whereby energies, other than the purely physical, are brought into play.

In giving some examples of the different ways in which healing works, my intention is not at all to advocate my own part in the process. It is expressly to illustrate the many different levels which are reached and touched when we allow ourselves to become a catalyst in the situation as we begin to work with these energies. The energy which flows through the healer's hands finds its expression in a manner and form which is appropriate in each case. We must never make a promise which is not ours to give. But always we must keep ourselves open and alert to the guidance of intuition which may ask us to work and act in a certain way.

One day, a person who felt very depleted and exhausted from a spell of overwork came for a treatment. There was nothing of a medical nature wrong. Afterwards he said he could feel energy flowing as though he was being recharged and balanced. Energy was being restored and, as he put it in his own words, he felt 'renewed and together again'. It was that spontaneous comment of 'being connected' used quite naturally.

Sometimes things are not without their amusing side also. One day a business friend, who was very successful both at home and abroad, rushed in and asked me to give him 'a quick blast' as he had to go to a most important meeting! Although he was familiar with our work, he had not felt inclined to become actively involved in any way. Afterwards, he was kind enough to come back to say that the meeting had gone extremely well and that he was very pleased with the results. So, once more, it was demonstrated that we function better when we are cool, calm and collected — or connected. Working with these energies in this way can help to keep us in a state of balance, can, in a sense, be used as a form of preventive maintenance.

Working with many people who lead busy lives, it is especially noticeable whether they are using predominantly their left brain or right brain. The level of activity can be felt as heat or warmth coming from that area of the head. A person who is working all day long in the office with figures or at a computer will tend to be using the left brain, that part which has to do with logical reasoning capacities. Conversely, perhaps, a mother who has been minding the children all day long and whose state of awareness is heightened, will be using her right brain. The right brain is the area of intuitive action. Sometimes the level of heat seems so intense that it is almost as though a circuit or fuse has blown. By using our hands, it is possible to bring down these energies, to calm and cool them. Also in this way, we are helping to bring about a balance between left and right brain activity, which is the way we should naturally function.

However, of course, these energies can also bring about healing in a very real sense by curing physical disabilities. Whilst it may not be possible to cure all ailments, for one reason or another, we must never restrict the possibility of being able at least to ease every condition. At a very practical level, a person wrote a letter of thanks '... for wonderful quick results from your healing of that sore on my face ... I could feel all that energy pouring into me so I wasn't totally surprised!' Here again we get evidence of a very real sensation of energy flowing.

The energies which are flowing may not, however, always be felt because a great deal of work may be taking place at a level other than the physical. When my wife, Elizabeth, and I were abroad on the continent one time, I was asked to give a healing treatment to the mother of a friend but, because of difference in language, we could not communicate with one another, so no conversation took place. Afterwards, we received a letter from our friend to let us know that the pain in her mother's lungs had ceased and that she could now breathe more easily. Also '... that she now prays every night — which she has never done before.' Because of difficulty in communication, nothing was said about prayer, yet this was the level which was touched.

One of the happiest incidents occurred when a friend rang one day to say that an aunt from England was coming over to stay for a short holiday and could they bring her for a treatment. So an appointment was made and in due course of time, the day arrived. The person concerned was about seventy and had great difficulty in getting up the two flights of stone steps that lead to the hall door. She walked with a stick; well, walk is not really the right description, for she could only put one foot forward and then bring the other up to it. She was very stiff and obviously any movement caused her great pain.

Sitting on the chair, she told me that she was taking pain-killers to ease the pain in her hip and in bed at night everything ached so much that she was also taking sleeping pills to try and help her sleep. The doctors had told her that there was nothing more they could do for her. She even found it difficult to get up from a chair and took two or three attempts before she could stand. Anyway, I gave her a treatment but felt that I would like to have done more. However, it would have been quite impossible for her to lie on a couch for massage or anything of that sort. So, at the end, I said if she would like to come back again the following week: if she thought it would be of any help, she would be very welcome to do so.

The following week, a relative brought her in again and she seemed to be somewhat better. I gave her another treatment and at the end, I felt impelled to take her by the arm and try to gently walk her around the room. Naturally, she felt a little nervous without her stick and moved slowly and hesitantly, one foot forward and then bringing the other one up to it in the usual way. After two or three rounds, I asked her to try and walk normally, with me still holding her arm firmly. Very slowly, she walked one foot after the other a few times around the room. I said goodbye, as she was returning to England, and saw them out, watching them as they went. Down the first flight of steps, she went in the usual way, one step at a time, but when they reached the level area before the second flight, she walked across it left, right, left, right in the correct fashion, but slowly, and then down the last flight of steps one, two, three, four ... to the bottom and out into the street. I closed the door gently and with a great sense of pleasure.

Then, about six months later, I received a letter from her, 'Dear Bill — she always called me Bill! — I have just arrived back to where I left over six months ago, you must think me mad ... I go for a walk every day, I haven't any pain and I feel fine'. She had, apparently, been all around the place visiting friends and relations. Much later I met her niece who had arranged for her to see me in the first place and she told me that at the end of her stay with them she had refused point blank to take her walking stick with her, as she now had no need of it.

More and more people are seeking alternative therapies in place of orthodox medicine. They have become disenchanted with the often aggressive nature of some of the so-called cures. Particularly so is this the case with many of the drug-based treatments where the side effects are often harmful and unpleasant, and sometimes conditions are set up where the body becomes dependent upon the drug for its survival. In a sense, all that has taken place is that the body has been offered an alternative disharmony. In the midst of the wonderful technological and scientific developments of modern medicine, all too often the body is treated in a purely mechanistic way, as though it were merely an object devoid of any feeling and spiritual content. It is this fact, perhaps, more than any other that has turned people to look for a more gentle and natural approach to health and healing.

If the best is to be achieved, it is essential that orthodox medicine and the so-called alternative therapies, such as spiritual healing, go forward together, hand in hand. Both sides must think and work continually in the sense of being complementary to, and not in competition with, each other, for both have much to offer. Always the patient must come first, and it must never be forgotten that we are spiritual beings in a material world. The healing process must include all three aspects — body, mind, spirit.

3

THE TAPESTRY OF LIFE

Every story demands a beginning and seeks an end: and so it is with life itself. Where did we come from? Where are we going? Where are we now? These are all questions we ask ourselves at some time or another. They are as relevant today as they were ages ago, back to the dawn of time. Who are we? Who do we become? These thoughts arise within the consciousness of every thinking person, and it is important that, so far as possible, we try to grasp some understanding of them, if our lives are to have any sort of meaning and order and purpose. An understanding of our relationship with ourselves, with each other and with the universe is important within the healing process; and especially so in the case of those who may become healers so that they may guide those who come to them for help. It is the task of the healer to try and bring about a harmonious relationship of the person with themselves, God and the universe; a balancing and integration within the cosmos.

If we are to find an answer to these things we must keep an open mind and have a vision of the future for creation is not static, but forever forward looking. There never was a time when we did not have available to us keys to unlock some of the mysteries of creation. Ever since the advent of humanity on the earth we have never been without guidance. Always there have been great teachers who came down to earth as 'Way-Showers' to light a path, show the way, and raise the consciousness and understanding of the people. These great and illumined souls dwelt in different places upon the earth, over different periods of time. With retrospect, we can see that they each brought a teaching suited to the needs of the particular people and country of the moment, and also in line with the evolutionary plan for the planet itself. Many of the various world religions grew out of those teachings, which were preserved within their tenets, and within the cultures of the different races. The word religion means the recognition of, and voluntary allegiance to, some power or presence greater than ourselves, that which we call God. Whilst the religions provided rules and guidelines by which the great mass of the people could live in harmony with each other, and with the great creative principle, there were, from time to time, also some to whom secret mysteries and ancient truths were divulged. The apostles, and those who were gathered around Jesus, constituted such a small but select mystery school. To the masses He would speak only in parables but when alone with His disciples he would open their understanding and explain the inner meaning to them (Mark 4:10–11):

> And when he was alone, those who were about him with the twelve asked him concerning the parables. And he said to them 'to you has been given the secret of the Kingdom of God, but for those outside, everything is in parables'

and again Mark 4:33–34

> with many such parables he spoke the word to them, as they were able to hear it. He did not speak to them without a parable, but privately to his own disciples he explained everything.

It was the duty of the priesthood to preserve and hand down these inner teachings from generation to generation, and to improve and raise themselves, through the knowledge they possessed. But religion was not always the friend of the state and, because of fear, their inner teachings were often submerged, lost and sometimes misunderstood. And religion itself felt in fear of losing power over its adherents if it broadcast too openly the Keys to the Kingdom of Heaven. So it was that the ancient truths were best of all preserved within the protective shelter of the mystery schools and secret organisations, which, from time to time, arose to bring their message, and then retreated from the scene, leaving behind a new impetus for mankind to ascend another rung of the ladder of evolution.

In the evolutionary scheme of affairs, we, the people of Planet Earth, have fallen far behind in our spiritual development and understanding, whilst, in a scientific sense, we have far outstripped our spiritual natures. This imbalance between the spiritual and the material needs much work to be done, both at a personal and collective level. There are many problems to work through, as is only too obvious from the violence and unrest to be seen everywhere today. It also means that many fixed dogmas and beliefs must be overcome, and an open mind entered into where new ideas, new thoughts and new concepts can take root and flower into a common understanding and acceptance throughout the planet.

Pressures from cosmic energies and other sources are already beginning to make themselves felt in the area of personal responsibility. For the first time in recorded history, people of all countries are being forced to co-operate and work together in a common undertaking, to protect the life of the planet.

Nature, and the environment itself, have forced us to pay attention to the delicate balance by which life itself, in all its forms, is both supported and preserved. When we align ourselves to spiritual law and take personal responsibility for our actions then the need for man-made laws disappears. This applies, not only at a collective level, but at a personal one also, where we take responsibility for our own state of physical, moral and spiritual well-being. Acting within the voluntarily assumed code of behaviour, we become our own judge and jury and walk hand in hand with the great march of creation. Our religion and way of life then become both personal and universal at the same time, as we live in harmony with God, the great cosmic principles and spiritual law. There have been cycles and waves in the life of the

36

planet where civilisation has reached great heights and
fallen away, only to arise again in an other place and repeat
the cycle. These rises and falls have been due to mankind not
learning the lessons of its incarnation and also the great disturbances and changes which have taken place in the earth's
surface, from time to time, necessitating a beginning, all over
again, by the remnants which have been left.

Today we stand upon the brink of the darkest age that
could yet befall mankind because of a possible nuclear holo-
caust and the persistent destruction of our finely balanced
environment, or, with a change of consciousness, upon the
edge of a new and wonderful dawn to herald in a golden
age. If we are to make the right choice there must be a rapid
change of consciousness and understanding, and an opening
of minds amongst people everywhere, and especially among
those who are the world's decision-makers. In this way, an
influence for good and progress in the right direction may
spread throughout the great mass of humanity; already there
is a growing body of concerned people in every country of
the world. A sense of global co-operation, brotherhood and
sisterhood, must somehow be instilled in the hearts and
minds of people everywhere.

Within our historical past, there have been occasions
when world thinking has had to be jolted out of a fixed belief, before it could advance further. The initiator responsible
for such an impulse usually ended up by being martyred,
but hopefully we have progressed beyond that stage today.
From a flat earth society in a literal way, through a geo-
centric concept of the universe, to a solar system of planets,
all required great changes within the consciousness of humanity; and yet they paved the way for future exploration and
understanding. Today we have taken our first few halting
footsteps into space and for the first time within recorded
history we have been able, as it were, to release ourselves
from the bonds of earth. The implications that this will have
are great and have yet to be felt. If we should abuse, in
anyway, the space surrounding our planet, as distinct from

its immediate environment, we may well find ourselves coming under stern discipline not of our own choosing. As we come to explore the planets and the stars, there is no knowing with what form of intelligent life we may come in contact, whether of an environmental nature, or of a more or less advanced degree of consciousness.

Today, more and more people are coming to an awareness of the continuity of consciousness, and the reality of more than one sojourn on the earth: that death does not extinguish the experiences of the past, or close the door on the opportunities and the responsibilities for the future. We reap the seeds that we sow, both the good and the bad. We are responsible for making amends for our errors of the past, and setting them right. Collectively we are the makers of history and we live the history we make. We will inherit the dreams of our visions if we will but give them life. Our thinking must become much more expansive to include the life on both sides of the veil and also to embrace, not only humankind as we know it, but also the angel, elemental and nature kingdoms, and other realms not normally perceived by our physical senses. The immediate need is for a concept which will integrate us with the life of the solar system and, through the solar consciousness, link us with the life of the universe and the word of God. It is of the utmost importance that we should continually strive to open our awareness to the co-existent and invisible states of consciousness which everywhere surround us and to our responsibility to them.

Civilisation today needs an impetus, a new impulse, to carry it forward into the age of change which is already upon us. We need to widen our horizons, extend our vision, expand our consciousness to embrace a larger comprehension of the wonderful universe in which we live and of which we are apart. This does not require that we abandon the old but, rather, that we carry it forward with us and give it new meaning and life. Like a master gardener, we must prune the old wood so that the new may grow and flourish. As Jesus told us, He came not to change the law but to fulfil it, and in fulfilling it He became the law, and added to it new precepts and a new law — the law of grace and love. Today our consciousness needs to be awakened once more. In times gone past the concept of God was a very impersonal one, a god of wrath and judgment, a god to be feared. This was, for a while, necessary in order that discipline and justice could be installed and instilled into the minds and lives of humanity. This was superseded by a very personal concept of God, a god of mercy and grace so that a balance might be achieved. Today, we need to inculcate a sense of reverence, respect and a feeling of rightness in all our actions. A reverence for All Things, literally; from the very atomic structure of our body to the great star systems of the galaxies, from the ground upon which we walk to the totality of the environment in which we live, we are a part of all these things and of each other. There is no such thing as separateness. We are all linked by the common thread of creation within the great tapestry of life. We must cultivate a sense of humility and acknowledgement towards an intelligence which is vastly superior to our own but which is only too ready and willing to guide us along the pathway of evolution and advancement — if we are but humble enough to listen and accept a helping hand.

Within the context of healing we should remember also that healer and patient are not separate, but connected, an integral part of the cosmos. By maintaining harmony with the universe we are better able to help one another.

4

THE HEAVENLY BEING

Ancient wisdom has handed down to us the dictum that 'Man contains within himself a blueprint of the universe'. Jewish mysticism maintained that 'God first created the Heavenly Man, the archetype, who filled the universe and served as the pattern on which it was made'.

To those who seek an understanding of their meaning, these two statements provide a key to help unlock the mystery of man himself and of his relationship to the universe. They have both an inner and an outer meaning, invisible and visible. We must learn to observe both objectively and subjectively, noticing similarities in the phenomena of the external world about us, with corresponding ones within our own being and body. In this way each will supplement the other so that, little by little, we will add to our total understanding, adding, as it were, building blocks of knowledge. The masters, and those gifted with heightened vision, confirm the truth of the comparison, so that others, who have not yet attained such levels of 'unfoldment', may safely use the key in their search for an understanding of self.

When we look up at the stars in the sky at night we behold a beauty and mystery that defies comprehension, and what we see in no way remotely reflects an image of how we imagine ourselves to be. And if we take a deeper look through the great telescopes of the astronomers, out into the great vastness of space, into the distant star galaxies and island universes of stars, we might be excused for thinking that law and order did not exist or that chaos reigned. For everywhere we look we see a headlong recession, or expansion, where every object is running away from everything else. At the limit of our observable horizon the speed of recession is such that it approaches the speed of light. One step further and it would become invisible and have no reality for us: the expanding universe of our astronomers, where great and powerful forces are at work but seemingly uncontrolled. But, coming a little closer to home, to our own solar system, we observe with awe and wonder the planets as they journey around the sun on the precise paths of their respective orbits, answering to the music of mathematics. They keep perfect track and course, repeating their circuits with unfailing accuracy and regularity through millennium after millennium, age after age: predictable, unchangeable. The serenity and precision displayed is such that there can be no doubt that law and order does exist here. It would be futile to question the absence of intelligent control. It is irrefutably demonstrated before our eyes.

One spring we took a short break and went to Greece and stayed on the coast some distance from Athens. Close by there was a small bay, from where we had an uninterrupted view across the ocean of the sun sinking below the horizon as it set. In the clear atmosphere there, the sunsets were magnificent.

One evening I walked down to the little bay in good time to watch the setting sun. Standing there, I watched as the sun slowly sank towards the distant horizon when, just a few moments before it touched it, there was a sudden change in my consciousness. As I looked and watched I felt the earth rise before me and lift upwards to meet the sun as it turned on its axis, its rim sweeping the face of the sun as it did so. Still feeling the earth turning beneath me as the sun disappeared from view, I became strongly aware of its immensity as it hung there suspended in space by some invisible and wonderful power. With an inner ear I seemed to hear a deep sound or rumble as it rotated on its axis. The feeling of standing there on this enormous globe poised majestically in space filled me with awe and wonder and a deep sense of humility.

Turning, I walked back in the growing dusk contemplating deeply what I had experienced.

Space itself may only appear to be empty and void, but, by inference, we can assume from the structures and patterns that we have observed and discovered that it also comes under the direction and control of a supreme intelligence. That same pattern of law and order, which exists at our microcosmic level, also exists out there in space on an immense macrocosmic scale.

Directing our observation from the macrocosm to the microcosm, from the infinitely large to the infinitely small, we find the same law and order displayed in the world of the atom. The sub-atomic particles of which the atom is composed exhibit the same pattern that is seen in the external world of space. The nucleus, or proton, represents the sun around which the electrons and neutrons circulate in precisely defined orbits. Except for scale, one is a replica of the other. Law and order are evident in both, and we cannot have law and order without intelligence. That same atomic structure exists within our own bodies.

Looking out into space once more at the great spiral nebulae, those wonderful star systems of spiral arms, extending from a central axis or nucleus, the whole majestically balanced and rotating about its central hub. At enormous distances from our home in the Milky Way galaxy they are beautiful to behold when seen enlarged on coloured photographic plates. If we look again at ourselves, this time with the aid of those who are clairvoyant, they tell us that they see the same pattern existing as part of an energy field surrounding us. This is often referred to as our etheric body, that subtle energy counterpart of the physical body. Within the etheric body are seen specific energy centres long known in the east as chakra centres, which we call centres of spiritual energy.* They are found over various parts of the body, and seven major ones serve the glands of the endocrine system and are connected to the corresponding parts of the spine, from the base to the top of the head.

Smaller chakras are linked to the feet, knees, hips and hands, elbows and shoulders, providing mobility and movement. There are also many minor, much smaller ones, all over the body where energy pathways cross. These points of energy constitute a matrix around which the physical body is draped. They are transformers of high energy from other dimensions, solar and cosmic, reducing them down to the specific vibratory levels or rates required by each of the organs, functions and processes of the physical body that they serve. They represent the power house by which the body operates, and should any of them not be functioning correctly, the corresponding bodily system will be affected accordingly. Bringing the over-active or under-active ones back into balance again is an important part of the healing mode. When all are operating in balance and harmony with each other, then the person enjoys a state of good health and well-being. They are interdimensional responding to our physical, mental, emotional and spiritual states of being. They are seen by clairvoyants to be rotating, and of different colours. The word chakra comes from the Sanskrit, meaning wheel, and it is interesting that both the astronomers and psychics use the same description for their observations saying that what they see are like whirling catherine wheels of coloured light.

At the mystery school in the Temple of Delphi there was a plaque over the portal on which were the words 'Man know thyself'. Somehow, deep within my consciousness, I seem to remember having been told that to these words they would add '... and then thou shalt know the gods and their energies'. This had a strong impact upon me and I often wondered of what energies they were speaking because we know they did not have oil, nuclear power, electricity or any of the other sources of power with which we are familiar.

However, if they were talking of their gods, they must have been speaking of powerful energies. They ascribed a god to each of the different forces of nature, believing that they were under the control and direction of an exalted being of high intelligence. They held that these energies were but specific manifestations of the numerous outpourings of the supreme deity, the source of all being. Again we have the injunction to look at ourselves.

One of the first discoveries made in the early days of our space flights was that the planet had a magnetic field. This was not anticipated and came as a great surprise. Named after its discoverer, the Van Allen radiation belts are extremely powerful fields of magnetic energy. Such a field or fields do not exist around the moon. We see here, perhaps, a similarity to the human aura, that magnetic field or cloak of many colours visible to seers, which envelops the person and may be detected with sensitive instrumentation. But we must be careful in our use of terminology. There are many electro-dynamic fields associated with living organisms and especially with the human body, and whilst some of these energies are undoubtedly magnetic in nature, there are some which are discernible to the healer and visible to the clairvoyant, which have yet to be classified scientifically. In due course of time, these very subtle energies, which have their origin at a supra-physical level, will be ascribed the place they deserve, when science can take the jump to include another dimension into the parameters of its thinking. It is, perhaps, significant that it has been found that astronauts suffer malfunction of the autonomic nervous system and depletion of their own magnetic fields when separated from the earth for any length of time.

So, we see space is not empty, but filled with unlimited energies, latent, apparently untamed, and in chaos. We cannot yet comprehend with our finite mind the organisation of these energies into some pattern and purpose by a supreme mind. Space is movement in action, creating continuously, expanding. The pattern of multiplication and expansion is inherent in all being. And so we have our expanding universe, the breath of God, one day to contract and recreate all things new.

Our sun is but a young star on the fringe of our island universe, the Milky Way galaxy, which is our home in space. In its journey around the heavens, as it traverses its great orbit about its parent sun, it is constantly collecting and transforming cosmic energy and re-radiating it in a form suitable for its family of planets. Within its centre is a spiritual sun which is the controlling force or element. All movement in space is a vortex. The great star systems as they rotate about their central hub or axis are also travelling along their plane of motion within the expanding universe. The planets, as they circulate around the sun, are also being carried along its great track as it, too, moves about its parent body. A rotary movement super-imposed upon a linear one produces a vortex. Evolution is the controlling and disciplining of those vortexes of energy movements.

The law and order of the solar system in which we live, and which also exists within our own body is but a sample of that same law and order which exists throughout the universe, and the whole of creation. Those distant star systems in the depth of space are functioning under the same universal laws but on an immeasurably greater scale. Orderliness is godliness.

The human body being then founded upon that same structure and pattern as we see displayed in the heavens, is designed to function upon that same system of orderliness and godliness. The stars and planets seem, somehow, to be rooted or locked into the melody or tune of this cosmic balance of law and order and cannot act outside of it.

Within the sub-atomic world we also find this need to maintain harmony and balance. It has been found in experiments with paired particles that one twin will appear to 'know' what is happening to the other. If the spin of one is changed, the other will instantly alter to maintain parity. If the electrical charge of one is reversed, the other will do likewise to maintain the balance.

In experiments, paired photons of light were fired in opposite directions and, whilst in mid flight, a polarising filter was placed in front of one of the detectors. No matter how the filter was changed, the photons remained strongly connected, so that the partner always knew what was happening to the other. As photons travel at the speed of light, information must somehow pass more quickly, or else there is another way of knowing.

In contrast to this, the human being has been given free will which gives us the freedom of choice, unlike the sub-atomic particles which appear to conform to some law that provides the tension necessary to maintain harmony and balance. In our own daily lives, we are constantly challenged to become conscious of, and conform to, this divine dance within ourselves, so that harmony may be preserved.

In today's world we are also subject to many man-made and other environmental and cosmic influences which affect our subtle body energies. By following our feelings and intuition, we can help ourselves to discriminate between those energies which are harmful to us, and those which benefit us. To do this, it is necessary, from time to time, to make space in our daily lives to be still and listen to this voice of inner guidance. By so doing, we contribute in our own way to the preservation of law and order within our own lives — to be truly in tune with the universal symphony.

* Recommended reading on this subject is one of Lilla Bek's books – *What Colour are you ...?*

5

THE LIVING BOOK OF NATURE

As we have seen, the different worlds or kingdoms, from the galaxies and stars down to the atom and its sub-atomic particles, have their own system of law and order, and function within that system. So too do we find that planet earth has its own set boundaries. It maintains harmony and rhythm by functioning within certain fixed cycles of day and night, and the four seasons, which provide periods of rest, fertility, growth and renewal. If the regularity of these cycles should be disturbed in any way, then the whole of life which the planet supports would be thrown into disarray. Life is programmed to respond to these cycles. We notice this particularly within the animal and vegetable kingdoms, in such ways as migrations, seed time and harvest time in crops, and even in the soil itself, for there is a time to reap and a time to sow. We too have our own bodily cycles and rhythms which are orientated to, and embedded, in the natural cycles of earth, sun and moon.

If, for instance, the 24–hour system should become irregular for any reason, our natural rhythm of rest, sleep and work would be completely disorganised. Should the seasons become irregular, nature would become disorientated and unable to adapt. It could adapt to a cyclical change but not to an irregular one. Regularity somehow is a pre-requisite for harmonious functioning, and we should perhaps pay more attention to this in our own lives than we do. The old adage 'Early to bed, early to rise' was certainly founded upon sound principles.

Already we can see changes in weather patterns, and the seasons are no longer clear-cut. Much of this change is due to the activities of the human race which has brought about disturbances in the balance of the environment, and within the earth itself. But some scientists are now finding that some of the planetary aberrations we experience such as earthquakes, freak weather patterns, electrical and electromagnetic abnormalities and even pathological changes in living organisms can be linked to changes in the solar system, the stars and the galaxy. The earth itself is affected by activity from outer space in its journey through the cosmos, as well as by the actions of humanity upon it.

In order to have experience within the earth plane, the soul requires a form, or vehicle, which will enable it to manifest and function so that it may fulfil its task, and this is, of course, the human body. Without it the soul would be unable to express itself and gain from its experiences on the earth. Our time here should be one of growth and expansion and should be a valuable opportunity not to be turned lightly aside or wasted. A large part of our work here is to learn to have respect for the planet and the world of nature that it supports, and which supports us. We have been given dominion over it and this means to be responsible for it and its well being. We must learn to work in harmony and to co-operate with it, and help it forward in its own evolutionary pattern. We are dependent upon one another, and we must realise that we are partners in the great scheme of life.

Just as the atomic worlds strive to maintain balance and harmony, so, too, does nature in its own way. We will find that if we continue to harm and destroy it then it will eventually rebel against us: for the tensions of harmony and balance cannot be stretched indefinitely. The rebound will be both catastrophic and painful as the natural forces act to reinstall harmony.

In the beginning, the organising by the supreme mind of the latent energies of space brought about the universe, and produced the sun and its elements, out of which our planet was spawned. Our planetary bodies have been conceived in the workshop of God, over a very long period of time, as we know it, and they contain all the elements of the earth. We have, therefore, that natural attunement with the earth itself and also with the sun. All the major components of the body – heart, lungs, organs, spine, etc – have been proven and tested from the most primitive of animal forms up to the 'man like' ape. It was with the perfection of the spine and with it the ability to stand erect that 'The Form' became ready to receive souls. It is the only form on earth to do so naturally.

There are, of course, two views regarding the origin of the human being, humankind, on the earth. One is the Darwinian theory of progressive and natural evolution. The other is the alternative view of esoteric thinking which pro-motes the idea that the Hu-Man form came into being, as a specific creation, when the time was right for souls to inhabit the earth. Always the search goes on for the missing link, that bridge between ape and man, but none is found. We do not today see apes evolving before our eyes into men. None, it seems, have made that intellectual jump. It would appear reasonable to side with the esoteric viewpoint that mankind did not descend from the ape, and neither did the ape evolve into man, but that the human being is a very special creation.

The idea of research and development is not a strange concept in our consciousness. It goes on all the time, and has done so since humanity began to make tools and fend for itself in a strange environment, for the earth is not the natural abode of the soul. We are accustomed, in our techno-logical world, to the process of development and refinement through experimentation. In the design and construction, for instance, of a space craft, the overall design is first drawn up and then the various parts and functions are built and tested in different laboratories. For example, the life support system would be the responsibility of one agency whilst the propulsion system would be that of another. The guidance system would become the task of yet another organisation, and so on for all the specialised components and systems. Finally, when all have been tested and proved they are brought together, for the first time, as a complete unit, and the prototype or form takes shape. As a result of experience gained through use, further improvement and refinement take place in an ongoing way, and so it is with nature and us. Our bodies today differ greatly from those of our fore-bears by the continual process of refinement and adaptation to suit environmental and cultural changes.

Just as the soul requires a form suitable for its use in the earth, we have a parallel situation when man wishes to function in an environment which is unnatural to him, such as beneath the water or up in space. Before being able to descend to the sea bed, a diver has to don a cumbersome suit designed to withstand the enormous pressures far below the surface. It has also to provide him with breathing apparatus and illumination in order to be able to see in the darkness of the depths. Similarly, an astronaut, when up in space, re-quires protection against the harmful unfiltered solar radiat-ions, and a pressurised suit to nullify the effects of zero gravity and the vacuum of space. In the same way, the soul has to attire itself when it comes down to earth. It has to take on what at first must seem to be a cumbersome suit of clothes in an unfamiliar environment. But we must rem-ember our body is our best friend — for all of our life. It will serve us truly and well for as long as we need it, provided we give it a chance.

In our evolution within consciousness, we have for-gotten that our body is a friend. It is not an enemy. We must learn to talk to it and encourage it in the same way that we talk to plants and flowers, and it will respond. It can be very helpful before an operation actually to talk to our body and explain exactly what is going to take place and the reason for it. This will greatly lessen the traumatic shock to the system from surgery, for instance, and other invasive treatments.

The body contains many different energies and ele-ments, and we must not be in conflict with them. We have seen in chapter 2, how if we do not live in harmony with them, dis-ease reigns which, if allowed to continue unchecked, becomes disease or illness. We must come to understand and accept the individual limitations of our bodies, and not to fight against them. Through acceptance we can raise the ideal and transcend the limitations which will fall away behind. We must not regret the mistakes of the past but look upon them as tools of the future. It does not matter so much that we make a mistake provided we profit by the experience and do not make the same mistake again. It is the consciousness, not the body, that is the cause of health or ill-health. The body is the victim, the casualty – not the cause.

Our body is constantly renewing itself. It is a known fact that the different cell-types (e.g. liver, skin, blood, etc) are continuously replacing themselves at different rates; and it is my understanding and belief that the whole body is replaced every seven years. It is important, therefore, to provide the best possible conditions that will prove fruitful for the body to grow in and to develop and evolve. This we can do by taking care of our physical health through good food, fresh air and exercise; and also by paying attention to our mental, emotional and spiritual health. In this way, we can create the right environment to help the body

We are a people with a planetary body containing all the elements of the earth. Anything that disturbs the planetary harmony in any way will have a corresponding effect upon our own body harmony. The natural state of equilibrium of the ecological system which has taken millions upon millions of years to establish and stabilise, is threatened with irreparable damage, due to a lack of appreciation and understanding by our present civilisation over a period of a few decades. It is only with the advent of our modern technological age that the balance of nature has been placed in such jeopardy. A situation which, if allowed to continue unchecked, will have devastating effects upon the human race and the planet itself. We have steadily distanced ourselves from the natural world of which we are inescapably a part. In olden times, people were much more keenly aware of their dependence upon the world of nature, and treated it with the respect and reverence that it deserved. They were very conscious of the signs they could read in the weather patterns in the sky, and in the movements and activities of birds and animals; all of which heralded some impending change in their environment, with its consequent affect upon their own individual lives. Daily they 'read the living book of nature' for what it had to tell them, and they were closely attuned to the life of the planet and the life which it supported.

The planet has feeling and consciousness and lives in harmony with the natural rhythms of sun, sea, air and rivers. If the natural balance of the reciprocal exchanges of those elements is disturbed, then the planet will suffer. Pollution today lies not only in the soil, the lakes, the seas and rivers but also in the atmosphere. The pollution of the atmosphere is not only of a physical and chemical nature, but also of a mental one. The very thoughts, both hidden and expressed, of mankind, affect the growth and development of the human, animal and vegetable, and even mineral kingdoms. The 'atmosphere' of the earth is in close communication with that of the sun and other planets. Any irregularity in it will be felt by the other bodies. Consequently, the earth will not only be affected directly by the disturbances within its own atmosphere, but also indirectly by the secondary effects caused through the distortion of the pure radiations of the other planets and the sun.

There is no assurance that evolution is ever upward by gradually increasing steps, and we stand today at a position which is very delicately balanced between progress and disaster. The New Age will most certainly arise out of the old — but what it will be depends upon what we make of it now. It has taken millions of years, by our time, to evolve the planet's support system to the present level, but we could destroy it in a generation through carelessness. If this should happen, then life would be withdrawn to the border-land to await incarnation at some time in the remote future, after the planet has been cleansed and prepared anew. Soul evolution could not run the risk of dangerous or damaging mutations which would serve no useful purpose for the growth and advancement of individual souls.

In Switzerland and Germany a third of the trees are either dead or dying due to acid rain which is carried by winds from the origin or source of its production, some of which lie outside the control of these countries. Also, many of their rivers are badly polluted by chemical effluents. Both of these countries have a very high awareness of the need to protect the atmosphere and the environment, and are taking steps to tackle the problem by the introduction of strict controls over damaging emissions. Further afield, the great tropical rain forests which cover approximately 7% of the earth's land surface are being destroyed at a rate of approximately 27 million acres a year. To put a scale on this figure it is equivalent to about an area the size of 30 football pitches a minute. Apart from the loss of the wonderful variety of plants and wild life that this represents, up to 40% of our medicines have their origin in tropical forest plants.

Above the planet itself, in the upper reaches of the atmosphere, the toll of man's activities is also having its effect. The ozone layer in the stratosphere is in increasing peril from chemicals, such as chlorofluorocarbons (used in aerosols) causing it to suffer a serious depletion of its level, which will result in an increase in the amount of ultra violet radiation reaching the ground. This, in turn, is damaging to life. On the other hand, industrial activity is increasing the concentration of ozone at ground level by as much as 30%. All of this is resulting in a rise in the temperature of the lower atmosphere, thus increasing the 'greenhouse' effect which traps heat near the ground, and a cooling of the stratosphere. No one quite knows how this change in vertical temperature differentials will affect the world's weather patterns.

Whilst this is of concern to us globally, it also has an affect upon us individually in a more indirect way. Some people are much more sensitive than others in their relationship to the elements, such as having an affinity with the air, earth or water; but everyone, to a greater or lesser degree, is connected with these elements. The trees are the lungs of the planet and are as much dependent upon a clean and pure atmosphere as we are. Any damage that they may suffer will be felt by people with a weakness in their respiratory systems. The rivers are the life blood of the earth and, similarly, anyone with disorders in their circulatory systems will be influenced by water pollution. Underground eruptions caused by atomic test explosions may very well bring a tendency to skin conditions arising from beneath. A sensitive balance exists between man, nature and planet and unless this can be reinstated, and a natural harmony reintroduced, the evolution of the human race is at risk. We face the prospect of trying to live in a semi-sterile and hostile environment. Through our incarnation, we should leave the planet a better place for our having been here, and return to that place from which we came a more evolved personality, because of our experience and endeavours. Unfortunately, our present generation is leaving the planet in a worse condition than when we came in, and many of us go back at a lower level of growth than when we arrived. We must remember that we borrow the earth and its bounty from our heirs and not from our ancestors.

We cannot harm the environment without harming ourselves. Improve it and we improve the quality of our own lives and those who follow after.

The affinity of the body to the elements and the environment is a most important aspect within the healing process.

6

THE COSMIC CONNECTION

Assimilation is at many levels — physical, mental, emotional and spiritual; and according to the level to which the receptivity is tuned, so will be the supply. We are aware, of course, of the nourishment that we receive at a physical level through assimilation of food, water and air but we are not so conscious, perhaps, of the fact that the assimilation is also taking place at the other levels at the same time.

Our mind is like a radio set, and is in tune with whatever we direct it to. Should we switch on a radio set, it will automatically pick up the last station to which it was tuned, which may be London, New York, Moscow or wherever. We have made a random choice, and should we want something different we have to retune the set and programme it accordingly. Our minds are like that and whenever we are not actively or consciously using them, they will tend to be receptive to just that area of thought in which they were last working. It is for this reason that it is so important to keep control of our thoughts, and in our 'free wheeling' modes, as it were, consciously to channel them into some area of creative activity. Should we be feeling angry, for instance, or have just had a row with someone, and we straightaway go out into a public place we will be receptive to all similar incoming signals from other people, if we have not first cleared our minds beforehand. But, worse still, we will be spreading those thoughts far and wide to other people, who will be affected in a similar way. So we can see that from a single incident many other people may be influenced unknowingly, and our own situation greatly aggravated by not having control of our thoughts. In the same vein, to sit and watch the late night horror film on television is just about the worst thing we can do if we want a peaceful night's sleep. Far better to read a few pages of some enlightening book, or listen to a piece of good music.

Our emotions also work in a similar fashion, and we know, for instance, that fear is contagious. Hysteria can quickly become mass hysteria when a crowd of people react together. Very often, an illness can be contracted through fear. It is the fear of the fear. That very thing which we dread may very well manifest if we dwell upon it too much. Consequently, we must try to keep a positive outlook in all such matters for good emotional health.

So far as our spiritual attunement is concerned, we should take care that it is more than just a one-day-a-week event. Our whole lives can be greatly enriched by bringing a spiritual aspect into all our affairs. We can turn many a menial task into a work of art, or carry out some uninteresting job in a spirit of service, such that others may also benefit, or gain by our efforts, as well as ourselves. By being constantly aware of our spiritual nature, we place ourselves in tune with the divine world and the help that it can bring us.

Our growth depends upon our keeping an ear open to the universe, keeping our personal radar open and in a state of expectancy; for space is full of mind. The planet and all the living and growing things evolved through the assimilation of intuitive impulses. A sort of impregnation of the atmosphere of the planet from higher guiding intelligence.

There is an old adage — 'As above, so below' — and perhaps we might add 'but just a little less'. In other words, there already exists at another dimension all that we have here. All the great inventions are not the product of our own conception. They were given to us from above in the form of impressions and intuitive insights. Those people working in a specific field already had their mind tuned in that direction and were ready to receive the seeds that were sown from above. The idea is not the prerogative of any one individual. It is often found that virtually the same invention is lodged in the patent offices around the world at the same time, so that a person wonders how it is that another has got hold of their idea. In a sense the idea was not their's in the first place.

Some of the great inventions and intellectual concepts, such as Einstein's theory of relativity, were not the result of logical deductions or reasoning, but were specific leaps or jumps in the process of thought. There is a way of knowing other than by reasoning or pure logical deduction, or by being told or taught by somebody else. There is a way of 'knowing' by tapping into or tuning into some level of consciousness where the thought already exists. In this way, new ideas may be brought into being by a direct process of intuitive thinking.

We must keep our minds open to the inflow of new ideas and systems which flow to us, from time to time, from the higher worlds. They come to us as conceptual impulses and influences, guiding our cultural, spiritual and technical evolution. We can see that there are great eras in our history in the form of art, music, architecture, medicine, science, religion, and so forth, where activity was high and attention focused upon these particular fields.

Today, following upon the industrial revolution of the last century, we are in the midst of a technological age. One of the main areas where developments are growing rapidly is in the realm of communication. It is possible now for people individually to have contact with each other virtually wherever they are in the world. This will have the result of bringing people closer together, so that the spirit of community will grow and no longer will there be the sense of isolation. But this also asks of us a certain responsibility in how we think and act, for no longer is it possible to make an arbitrary decision without it also affecting someone else at the same time. Already we can see this happening in the world at large, for should any nation act arbitrarily, either politically or economically, it has global repercussions. The closer we draw together, the more we are affected by each other's actions, physically, mentally and emotionally, and we must always keep this in mind.

Already we have assimilated many of the impulses of the Aquarian Age, such as new forms of power and energy. We must learn to use them generously and creatively and not destructively. Nations must work together in harmony, for the benefit of the world at large, and the exploitation of none. We are in a time of transition as we move from one age into another. Already the nations have moved much more closely together, but there are still many of the old destructive forces at work. Individually we must become aware of this higher guiding intelligence, and consciously co-operate and work with it. In this way we make ourselves open to receive new insights into every aspect of life, and the way forward.

That we are subject to outside planetary influences has long been the subject of debate. There is no question that, at certain physical levels, we are affected by such things as solar flares, sunspot activity and the effects they have upon our environment, and the phases of the moon upon the tides. But at a more subtle level we are also subject to solar, planetary and cosmic energies of which we are not so readily aware. Not that these control us in any way, but rather, once we begin to sense their activity, we can begin to understand why we react and feel in certain ways at different times, and respond accordingly. The changing influences, as we move out of the Piscean and into the Aquarian Age, and traverse a different part of the heavens, will be marked by a raising of the energies that will tend to heighten our sensitivity and awareness, and bring about a sense of unification and puri- fication. The tendency will be for humanity to become one with each other, with our environment, and with the uni- verse. The many groups which today work for peace and healing, through prayer and meditation, can gain extra strength by linking with one another in thought and also by attuning to, and working with, the powerful energies which are being beamed upon them, from the cosmos, at the present time.

The New Age is opening before us and we are living in its dawning. In the fast moving world of today, change is an element that is constantly at work in our lives. This can be good, for out of the old the new is born. We must be careful not to indulge in change for the sake of change, lest the wealth and experience contained within that which has been lightly cast aside will be irretrievably lost. There are good reasons why the ladder of ascension must be maintained intact and climbed, rung by rung. But we cannot stand still, for progression and evolution imply movement, and that which remains static dies. This requires that we keep our minds open, flexible and ready and willing to accept the ideas of the future which impress themselves strongly upon us from time to time. They will sometimes necessitate that we relinquish something of the past in order that we may embrace that which is new.

This same quality of change is very evident in the sphere of health. More and more people are seeking alternative therapies, and a more gentle and natural approach, in place of orthodox medicine. The shadow of the future indicates that the way forward will be through the integration of medicine, healing and spiritual understanding. Waiting to be developed are many more wonderful methods of diagnosis and treatment, through the subtle energy fields which surround and are a part of the body itself. All these things will unfold themselves in due course of time, when we can open ourselves to understand that they can be so. In our time it is for us to read daily the Cosmic Book of Life.

7

VIBRATION
Identity through Attunement

We are electrical by nature, from the electro-chemical reactions of the minute cell to that magnetic sheath, the Aura, the cloak of many colours, that surrounds us; from the electrical nerve pathways and the electrical currents produced by muscle activity to the heart and brain wave patterns measured by ECG and EEG machines. Electricity dominates, controls and maintains our life. It is the great secret and sacred force of creation — the one force from which everything descends.

All energy stems from the one primal source, but there are many subtle extensions of this single energy which manifest at different rates or frequencies. Each rate or frequency has a unique vibrational pattern and corresponds to a specific aspect of the many countless facets of creation. Thus the difference between one atom and another is one of frequency, a rate of vibration. The atomic world is an enigma, in that when looked at from one viewpoint it gives the appearance of being solid, of having solidity. On the other hand, to modern atom physics, all things may be reduced to vibration, rhythm and frequency. Light and other forms of energy have a dual character, behaving, at times, either as a particle or as a wave — a solid particle in the concrete world of matter, or a wave form in the relatively vast nebulous regions of the inner space of the atom.

The combining of different atoms produces an element. For example, hydrogen and oxygen when combined together in the proportion 2:1 produce water H_2O. This blending of two different but unique substances is but a harmonising of two different rates of vibration to produce a new 'note' having its own individual pattern of vibration. It is for this reason that the production of atomic energy by destruction — by fission — is so wrong. The shattering of the sacred forces is the complete antithesis of creation, and the harmful and damaging effects of the residue of the reaction pose a danger for mankind, not only in this generation, but for many to come. We are acting in a most irresponsible manner by passing on to our successors the problem of dealing with the highly lethal waste products that we ourselves are unable to handle now.

The Chernobyl accident was a signpost along the way, and of concern to all who are interested in preserving and improving the health of the environment and of ourselves. There are still diverging views within Russia itself as to whether the town of Chernobyl, about eleven miles from the nuclear power station, should be demolished or not. The atomic energy ministry wants the radioactivity hit town to be destroyed, whilst the official political view is to encourage more people to resettle in decontaminated towns and villages within eighteen miles of the power station. Like many other difficult environmental and other problems today, they tend to become political issues.

It would be far better to put the generation of atomic energy by fission to one side, and devote all our efforts and funds to trying to develop nuclear power by fusion; by the marrying of the creative forces of the atom to produce a clean reaction. Love is the binding force in all things. The amount of love that is put into anything determines its life, its duration, whether it be our clothes, our home or our relationships. Love is God in action, the cement of the universe.

Whilst function within a frequency range is a criterion of matter, it is also true of the more subtle manifestations such as sound, colour, light, gravity, etc. All these operate within specific wave bands or energy levels, and in so far as they are a part of the material world, are locked into or confined, as it were, within set boundaries. Outside of these boundaries they do not manifest of their kind to us at a physical level. They do, however, have their counterparts in the more subtle worlds, but, unless the physical form is tuned to these higher frequencies, they are neither discernible to it nor a part of its experience.

When we come to know more about and understand these various higher energy levels we will be able, for instance, to use gravity, or gravitational forces, instead of having to fight or overcome them in our efforts to move from place to place.

It is to these various energies that the individual bodily functions and organs are tuned by the soul operating through the chakras, or spiritual centres, and the repetitional functional areas. Thus, the heart, lungs and other organs are in resonance with the individual frequency ranges to which they respond, in much the same way that a wireless set may be tuned, by a process of selectivity, to different incoming signals, which are all present at the same time.

The repetitional functions are those that keep the body working and functioning without our conscious knowledge. They control such processes as respiration, circulation, digestion, assimilation and elimination and provide us with the luxury of living without conscious effort. Working continuously they keep the basic body systems operating whether the person is awake or asleep. Tuned as they are to these higher energy rhythms, they can be very easily upset by certain yogic and other practices, such as unusual breathing patterns and exercises, and control of heartbeat activity. Unless the person is well balanced and in a state of good health, they should not be taken up unless under the direction of a skilled and experienced teacher. The repetitional functions should not be interfered with, and if any of them are taken over and placed under conscious control, then it can become very dangerous, as it is extremely difficult to hand them back again to the subconscious level, and to reinstate the natural rhythms. It is for this reason that we should keep, as far as possible, to our natural body rhythms, and abide by this key for good health — physical, mental, emotional and even spiritual.

The existence of bio-rhythms is well known nowadays. Many organisations, where their personnel are engaged in work of an extremely demanding nature, or where the safety of the activity is paramount, such as in public transportation, pay particular attention to them. Some airlines and railway authorities schedule their work rosters so that pilots and train drivers are not asked to work on days where their bio-rhythms are low. Superimposed on our 24–hour biological clock these physical, emotional and mental rhythms have 23, 28 and 33 day cycles respectively. When all peak together we may feel 'on top of the world' and capable of anything, but when all the troughs occur together it is a day to take it easy, if we can. These cycles are plotted from the day of birth. Small pocket calculators have been produced so that one can see, at a glance, in what particular phase of our cycles we are for any given day.

Whilst it is not good to let these things rule our lives we can, by turning the coin, as it were, let our bodies speak to us instead of our speaking to them. Just as we can learn to speak to our bodies, we can train ourselves to be quiet and listen and let them speak to us. We know that there are days when we feel very alert mentally but our physical body does not feel like being pushed; a day to catch up with correspondence, or work out details of that plan that we have been talking about for so long. Or, perhaps, another day we may feel that we just cannot bring our mind to concentrate but that we would love to be out and about; a day to chop the wood, dig the garden or build a wall. In this ordered and regulated world, we cannot always do just as we please, but with a little feeling and insight we can often adjust work, or home routines, a bit to suit our moods. In this way, bio-rhythms can become a map or guideline in our activities, and not a burden or mystery as to why we feel that way. Once we have experienced this ourselves we can teach others to feel into life in the same way and thus help themselves. On one small workshop, of two weeks duration, that we attended, there was a remarkably high correspondence of compatibility of the bio-rhythms of the group. Everyone jelled very quickly, and got on well with great harmony and enjoyment.

Everything has a pulse, a beat, from the smallest atom to the earth itself. The sun's approximately eleven year cycle of sunspot activity is well known, but astronomers were surprised when researchers discovered, from geological readings, that the sun has maintained a steady beat of 11.2 years for over 600 million years — truly a cosmic pulse. The earth is like a giant bell suspended in space as it sounds its deep tone pulsating with a beat of 69 times every twenty-four hours. The stars and galaxies pulsate in a great symphony of movement. We all have our own sound, that note which is unique to us and with which we each ring.

We can learn to recognise our own sound, and respond to it by listening to the tone of our voice as we speak, as it resonates our own note. To become in tune with this note, and to hum it quietly to ourselves, from time to time, will help to integrate and hold our physical form and to inculcate a sense of well-being within us. We know how when we listen to certain pieces of good music it will thrill our very bodies. A vibration will run up and down our spine and flow outwards throughout our whole being. That beautiful piece of music evokes, from the very depth of ourselves, a resonance or response which strikes a chord with our own unique note. Just as colours affect people in different ways, so do we each harmonise with our own particular vibration, colour and sound.

Sound can be used for healing, but it can also destroy and damage if used wrongly. Certain sounds and music of a given pitch and volume, can shatter and harm the subtle bonding force which holds our physical bodies together. Music of a certain beat can raise and stimulate energies. Many tribes played certain rhythmic music, and engaged in dances which raised the aggressive side of their nature, and depressed their sense of fear before going into battle. When directed mentally by those who knew how, the music of the drums also sowed the seeds of fear into the hearts and minds of the opposing side who heard the sounds from afar.

However, music can also be a beautiful therapy, both for healer and patient. It is good to meet in a small group for this purpose, and to sing together certain songs of an uplifting kind, such as Gregorian chants and other music, that will link us spiritually with our higher self. It is important for all to participate, for it is the act of bringing forth the sound from deep within ourselves that is so stimulating. We can listen externally while, at the same time, we make music internally. If we do not have anyone who can lead the group, we can play recorded cassettes, even making up our own choice of selections. It is good to prepare well beforehand so that the atmosphere is conducive to what we wish to achieve. Soft lighting, candles, flowers and gentle aromatic fragrances can all help to create the right environment. Perhaps we may be able to get permission to use a local church, from time to time, for this purpose, if this feels good. Once when we were singing in this way some visitors came in to look around the church. They quietly sat and joined us for a while, and then, just as quietly, left.

In one hospital, a doctor noticed that patients in a particular wing always seemed to recover and get well more quickly than in other parts of the hospital. When he investigated, he found that there was a church nearby which had a very active choir which used to practise frequently. The sound of their singing could be heard by the patients in this particular wing, and he concluded, that it was that which had a beneficial effect and helped to speed their recovery.

Song therapy is uplifting, renewing and revitalising for all who participate. It helps to raise the vibrations of our physical body, and strengthen its bond at an atomic level, and integrate us with our spiritual nature. We are each a note in the symphony of the universe.

As we have seen there are subtle connections between light, colour, sound and aroma through their vibrations. A person's perception of these things can take place at more than one level at the same time. For instance, an aroma will often conjure up a certain taste because of past associations. Or a taste will evoke a sense of colour because it 'feels' that way. Maybe a particular piece of music will bring to mind a scene comprising colour form and movement that we relate to in some way.

In the past we have had to rely upon our own intuitive awareness, or upon what psychics have told us, for an understanding of these subtle connections of different levels of vibrational activity. That somehow things only appear to be separate but that at a deeper level they are in some way connected, as we often realise from our own experiences. But now the truth that things are not separate has been confirmed for us by natural science from a realm that is not necessarily intuitive, with the discovery of the hologram. This scientific aspect can have meaning both for the healer and others as to how we relate to those subtle energy fields.

A hologram is a perfect three dimensional picture produced by means of laser light. It is possible to illuminate an object with laser light in such a way that two sets of light waves capture its image in the form of an interference pattern on photographic film. When a beam of laser light is projected through the developed film a perfect three dimensional picture is seen. It can be looked at from different angles as though one were actually walking around the object, while viewing it. But the most surprising thing is that if the negative is cut in half, or quarter, or even into smaller pieces, and a fragment is illuminated, a picture of the whole object appears, not just a part. The smaller the fragment the poorer the definition, naturally, but, nevertheless, the essence of the whole is there.

In another form a picture may be embedded into a glass amulet or pendant for instance — perhaps a rose or figurine of some sort. Should the glass be accidentally dropped or otherwise broken into many pieces, it will be found that all of the fragments will contain a picture of the whole, in miniature. So we find that holographic fragments carry the information or essence of the whole of which they are a part.

We can pursue this thought further and bring it close to home, for, in the same way, we have this holographic connection with the world around us. We are linked with the great principles of earth, air, fire and water, for we are composed of all of these elements. And it is through this holographic attunement that we find our own individual affinities with colours, sounds and fragrances — that happy resonance that makes once more for harmony and balance within ourselves.

The understanding of the holographic concept is of great importance because, when taken to its logical conclusion, we can see that every cell of our body contains the information of all the other cells. Whilst some are arranged in the different patterns of limbs and organs, muscles and nerves, all have been derived from the original seed, which contains the blueprint of the whole person. Perhaps it is through the hologram that we find a real analogy to the old idiom that 'man contains within himself a replica of the universe', and a confirmation of the old mystical idea that God first created the heavenly man who filled the universe and provided the pattern on which it was built. We truly are a holographic fragment of the universe and of each other. We contain within ourselves the essence of the whole, and it is this holographic bridge which links us together and with the universe.

> 'Where were you when I laid the foundation of the earth? ...
> when the morning stars sang together and all the sons of
> God shouted for joy?'
>
> JOB 38:11

8

THE AURA AND ITS COLOURS
A Living History

We speak of electromagnetic, electrodynamic and electro-static fields as if these are separate and different, but in reality they are but different manifestations of the one force – electricity in action. We measure them with different instruments but the observation depends upon the instrument that is being used. For instance we use an ammeter to measure the amount of current that is flowing, the number of amps; but we use a voltmeter if we need to know the voltage. One instrument will not serve both functions. Within the healing process we speak of magnetic energy, and the magnetic and gravity fields of the body but we must be careful not to limit their range by compartmentalising them, perhaps incorrectly, into too narrow parameters. That they are electrical in nature is certain. Just as a scientific instrument will detect or measure a specific function or activity that it has been designed to read so also do sensitives relate in their own way to the many different subtle energies in which we are immersed and which are a part of life. In their own way their perception and description of these different manifestations may not always agree with one another because of the individual manner in which their psychic attunement works and the level of its development. This is not to say that one description is right and another wrong, rather that each is describing it in the way that each sees it.

The aura, that cloak of many colours which surrounds us, has an electrical magnetic component and is a manifest-ation of our state of being at any given moment, being com-posed of the radiations of the physical, mental, emotional and spiritual aspects of ourselves. It is an indicator of the level of our evolution along the path of life. At the same time, potential illnesses and disharmonies also show up in the aura before their effects are seen at a physical level. In this way it can be a useful means of diagnosis for those who are able to detect or sense these signs, and treatment of the condition can be commenced before it has taken root within the body itself. The results of past illnesses or accidents also leave their mark upon the aura, and in this way it becomes a living history of the person, both past and into the future. It is constantly changing with our thoughts and moods and general state of health.

The aura is also a means of protection of the body itself. Should the magnetic energy be dispersed through shock, accident or extreme exposure, the body temperature will fall dangerously. The heat energy should be maintained artificially until the magnetic field is restored. At the same time it can act as a kind of radar by picking up in-coming signals from the world about us. In situations or places which are dangerous or unpleasant to the individual, it will contract strongly around the body in a protective manner. In a safe and pleasant atmosphere, such as with friends, it will expand, mingle and interchange with that of others. A successful actor or orator is able to expand his aura greatly so as to embrace his audience. In the same way, a patient will come within the aura of the healer when they are working together. And this is one reason why the healer must always hold himself, or herself, in as high a state as possible, physically, mentally, emotionally and spiritually so that the patient may benefit thereby. Should the healer be at a lower potential in any way, then the flow will be in a reverse direction. It has been shown, when patients are connected to an EEG machine, that their brain wave patterns take on the same steady relaxed state as that of the healer.

As described by most clairvoyants, the aura is composed of bands of different rainbow-like colours surrounding the body in the shape of an oval, and they each seem to have a specific meaning and influence.[1] The aura of an ideal person would appear white, as white light contains all the colours of the rainbow perfectly blended. However, we are not all perfect and therefore our auras show various colours according to our state of being at any given time. When the bands of colour are well-defined and clear-cut, a well-organised and disciplined life may be expected. It is when these energy fields become disorganised and unco-ordinated that their protective harmony breaks down causing tensions and areas of stress – sometimes of psycho-mental conditions, and even loss of spiritual direction. As we are spiritual beings in a material world the aura is a bi-dimensional phenomenon. It is an emanation from the soul shining through the consciousness and personality of the person. Should the consciousness of the personality in any way obstruct the light of the soul then the person is at risk in that area of life and lacks protection from the soul force itself.

Nearest the body is an energy field, like a grey mist, which is seen around all living things, plants, trees, animals and even mountains. This is the nature field which is sometimes referred to as the etheric counterpart of the body – the blueprint or matrix upon which the physical form is built. It is known, for instance, that if a salamander loses a limb it can grow another one. In following this line of thought, it has been possible to regrow a severed finger-tip, provided the finger is kept protected and not interfered with surgically. Even the original fingerprint patterns are reproduced. And, of course, we know that people who have had an amputation can still feel the 'phantom' finger or limb.

Kirlian photography demonstrates that there is an energy field surrounding all objects.[2] It is a way of producing a print or image of an object by subjecting it to a high voltage high-frequency electrical field. The object to be photographed is placed upon an insulated plate, within the instrument and subjected to the high tension field. The energy field of the object reacts with the electrical field of the apparatus itself to produce an interference pattern or corona-like effect. This is recorded on photographic paper so that emanation of light surrounding the object may be seen. In the case of a person, a photograph is taken of a hand or foot.

To a trained practitioner the photograph of a 'Kirlian aura' will give an indication of a person's physical and psychological state at any given time. The pattern of a corona of a sick person is different to that of a healthy person. But, perhaps, of even greater significance is the fact that experiments have shown that changes may be seen in the pattern of a corona prior to the onset of some illness or disease. Changes within the energy field itself often precede the manifestation of some illness or disharmony at a physical level. If developments continue successfully along these lines, examination of the Kirlian aura could become a valuable diagnostic tool, and provide an early warning of some irregularity within the person which needs attention.

The Kirlian camera is also being used successfully to investigate the life force energy of seeds, plants and food, etc. Crop samples can be examined to see if there are incipient signs of disease, and action taken accordingly. In other instances, photographs of a leaf will show a picture of its life force. If a portion of the leaf is cut off, and another photograph taken, the 'ghost' outline is still visible. Perhaps we see here a parallel to the phantom limb which can still be felt by amputees.

Sometimes in our own healing work we have felt, in our hands, an irregularity of energy over some part of the body, before there was any outward sign of a problem. Subsequent diagnosis by doctors at a later stage confirmed that there was a pathological condition which needed medical treatment.

The next field which is Red is the basic energy field, the animating creative one. It is the great creative force which energises all things. Representative of sex, pro-creation and the need to love and be loved, it is concerned with our senses and feelings and is an emotional area which can be troublesome to deal with. But it is the basic love force and when used wisely the person is generous and outgoing and enjoys well the good things of life.

After this comes Orange which is a mixture of Red and Yellow and displays the attributes of both.

The next field is Yellow which is the mental field, and shows the person's intellectual and mental capacity. It indicates the potential to grow and develop in this direction. It is the colour of study and a bright intellect and cheerful disposition. It is the living register of our thought life.

We then come to Green, that band of colour which is the astral or psycho/psychic realm. It acts as a bi-dimensional bridge linking the purely physical levels of consciousness which are restricted by third dimensional laws to the higher levels of consciousness from which intuitive feelings, sensations and intuitions can flow into the conscious mind. When the green astral field is strong it serves as a protective screen to the physical mind from the lower astral forces. If it should be weak or depleted then this opens the way to mental instability and even obsessions and mental disturbances of low psychic origin. It also provides us with our link with nature, the earth and the fertility of the planet in all its forms. Those people with 'green fingers' ...

The next field is the spiritual field which is a beautiful rich Royal Blue. When it is strong and radiant the spirit is able to protect, guide and steer its human partner safely through the many experiences of life and a good incarnation may be expected. Should the spiritual aspect of our nature be obstructed or frustrated in any way then we lose the protection of this beautiful field.

The last stage which is seldom visible, represents the deep resources of the spirit itself and its links with the cosmic and its divine origin. If it is seen it appears as a delicate Mauve or Purple gently outlining the whole aura, but mostly it is only just glimpsed here and there. It is a protection to the spirit itself as it draws close to the earth life of the soul which serves it and makes such a connection possible. But the home of the spirit is amongst the stars as it

experiences the endless wonders and delights of the universe for truly in our father's house there are many mans-
ions or dimensions.

Thus we see that the human being has existence on
several planes at the same time and provided that all these
energies are kept in balance, the soul enjoys a harmonious
and well-ordered life. The various shells of the aura represent the different vehicles or subtle-bodies, such as the
astral body or the mental body, that the soul uses as it experiences these different zones of consciousness.

Of all the solar and cosmic rays which beam upon us,
light occupies but a small window of that broad band of
electromagnetic radiation. Yet, without light we would not
know life as it exists on the planet today. Light literally is
our life-line. Furthermore, sunlight, which we so worship
and appreciate, contains all the colours of the spectrum. If
we pass sunlight through a prism it is refracted into bands of
colour ranging from red through orange, yellow, green, blue,
indigo and violet. Unaware of the fact we daily walk about
in an atmosphere of living colour. Also, perhaps more than
we realise, we are influenced by the colour of things around
us such as the colour of the clothes we wear, of the rooms in
which we live and work, and even by the colour of the food
we eat.

How does colour affect us, and why? Colour affects our
moods and feelings for better or for worse depending upon
our own individual colour make-up and the particular
colour in operation at the time. In one of the workshops that
we give on experiencing colour, it is interesting for a person
to be able to sit in a colour atmosphere and actually feel it
and how it affects them, and for the other people around to
observe the reactions. We use stained glass, which is a nice
medium to work with, in the form of slides and by means of
a projector, project the colour onto a screen in a darkened
room. The person sits on a chair sideways to the screen so
that they are not looking directly at the colour but sitting in
its atmosphere. With any given colour it will be found that

73

one person will only be able to sit there for a few moments before they become uncomfortable and restless, whereas another person will say that they could sit there all day. It is interesting for those who are watching to observe that when a person feels comfortable in a certain colour, the intensity of the illumination reflected from the screen is reduced, or at least neutral; whilst in the case of a person who is not happy with that particular colour the reflected intensity is often enhanced. In the one case the person is deficient in that colour and is absorbing it, but in the other case there is a surplus of the colour in the person's make-up and it is increasing the illumination.

We wear a coat of light, a cloak of many colours – the aura – that reflects our changing moods and state of being at any given time. Our thoughts and emotions greatly influence the colour tone and quality of our aura. The purer and higher our thoughts and aspirations, the more beautiful and colourful will be our aura. This is why colours affect us in different ways at different times; whether they harmonise and complement or clash with our colour atmosphere of the moment.

We have found in our work that it is very beneficial to combine spiritual healing with colour healing and in our own colour light healing sanctuary there is a screen which can be illuminated with either a single colour or combination of colours ranging from Red to Violet. It is nice to give treatments within the colour atmospheres chosen for the specific needs of the person at the time, and it is interesting that when asked to make a choice, a person will nearly always chose the colour best suited to their needs – they need that colour. So colour can bring another quality or dimension into the healing process. At other times the colours are changed regularly and never go out so that the sanctuary radiates its healing and peaceful atmosphere day and night.

Colour, sound, taste and smell are all closely related. Music produces the most beautiful harmonies of colour in the higher octaves above visible light. One of our friends, who is clairvoyant and a very good healer, had almost to be restrained when she was taken to her first symphony concert because she became so excited at the wonderful display of colours produced by the music; perfectly visible to her but quite unseen by her friends and those around her.

One day a person, whom I had not met before, made an appointment to come to see me. When the door-bell rang at the appointed time I went out into the hall to answer it. As I crossed the hallway I was met by a most beautiful perfume, even though the door was closed. Mentally, I prepared myself to meet someone whom I imagined to be elegant and well-dressed. When I opened the door, to my surprise, standing there was a very nice-looking woman but casually dressed in slacks and short-sleeved blouse. Later, as we talked about the reason for her coming, she said that she, amongst other things, was allergic to all forms of make-up and scent. She could use none of these things. She did not have to because her inner beauty shone through so brightly that the aroma of her own atmosphere was above all these things. We each have our own atmosphere of colour, sound, aroma and taste. It is important to preserve harmony in all these energy fields by only using those things which are compatible to them.

1. *ROBE OF MANY COLOURS*, R.P. Beesley — an excellent introduction to this subject. The interpretation of the meaning of the colours is founded upon his works.
2. *THE KIRLIAN AURA — Photographing the Galaxies of Life*, Stanley Krippner and Daniel Rubin; and *KIRLIAN PHOTOGRAPHY, RESEARCH AND PROSPECTS*, L. Gennaro; F. Guzzon, P. Marsigli.

9

HEALING TECHNIQUES

There are many different healing techniques. I am describing just one because it is a method that I was taught and learnt a long time ago, and have been using for very many years. It is a healing technique which is simple and requires no special preparation in the way of a room, or the use of any special equipment. It can be carried out anywhere, for people of all ages, old and young. It has the advantage that as one does not need to touch the patients they can remain fully dressed, and it is even possible to do it for someone in bed, or in hospital, if we have the permission to do so. In use it has proven to be both safe and beneficial.

The first stage in this particular healing technique is to balance the chakras/spiritual centres, by using the hands as conductors or connectors. By holding the hands just over, or gently upon the centres – working with a pair – the energy of a higher or overactive one may be fed into one of lower energy. Ideally all the centres should be evenly balanced, that is, they should each be functioning at their own specific rate. This can be felt by a uniformity of warmth. Also, when working in this way, high energy of a spiritual nature may flow through the healer's hands. This may be felt by the patient as either pleasantly warm, or very hot, or sometimes cool. The quality of the energy is modulated according to the need of the patient, and the area being worked upon, and takes place without conscious direction of the healer. For instance, an inflamed condition would require that heat be conducted away from the site, and not increased. Apart from balancing the energies of the spiritual centres, the hands may also be used to bring relief and healing by placing or holding them gently over, or upon, the area of the body needing treatment. Working in this way after an operation, we have seen the inflammation being drawn away from the site of surgery, just by passing a hand above and over the area, and have felt the heat come down. In this case, one would be working at an etheric level, and healing the tear in the etheric sheath.

To begin, the healer stands behind the patient who is sitting on a stool and places his/her hands upon the patient's shoulders. At this point, an attunement with the patient is made, and in each case the healer should always ask in prayer that the patient might receive that help and healing which is best for them at this time, not forgetting themselves that they might be a channel through which God's healing power may flow. It is good also to link with Christ and the healing angels. One should not concentrate too much, at first, upon what is wrong with the person, even if this is known, but leave the energies to flow naturally to touch the level that is needed. At this point, however, the healer may receive information intuitively that is important to pass on to the patient, and which may be relevant to them in the circumstances. But always great care, respect and discernment must be exercised as to how the information is imparted.

Then, with one hand held gently over the base chakra the other hand may be used to balance, in turn, the solar plexus, heart and thyroid. Then, with the hand that is over the thyroid held there, the other hand may be gently, and slowly, drawn up the spine to the back of the head at the nape of the neck. In this position, that hand links with the pituitary. While the hand is being drawn up the spine, energy changes may be felt at certain places, which will be an indication that nerve energy to the respective organs and body functions corresponding to that part of the spinal column is blocked. Or that there has been an injury to the spine or misalignment of some sort.

A pain in the back is often a magnetic tension or blockage at that particular place, and can be relieved in this way. After this part of the treatment, it will be found that the energy flow up the spine feels smooth and free. When the pituitary and thyroid have been balanced, the hand over the thyroid may be moved up and gently held over the forehead to balance the pineal or third eye centre. Finally, the crown chakra may be balanced with the pineal by using the hand which was dealing with the pituitary, and placing it over the crown of the head. All the spiritual centres should now be nicely balanced. With this treatment, always remember to move only one hand at a time so that connection is maintained.

The next step is to deal with the magnetic fields. There are two main fields functioning within the aura, the magnetic field and the gravity field, which are a very important part of the subtle anatomy of the person. These two fields should surround the body like well fitting cloaks, but in the stress and rush of everyday life, or in times of illness or accident of any kind, these two fields tend to separate. The tension of the magnetic field is upwards so that it tends to rise above the body, and appears to be linked to the higher levels of consciousness and our spiritual nature, whereas the pull of the gravity field is downwards, and its tendency is to slip on the body being connected with the earth, and also carrying a reflection of all our negative responses and conditions. The gravity field also links into all the drainage areas of the body. The balancing and harmonising of these magnetic fields has a very important part to play in the healing process, and in re-instating a sense of well-being within the person, but most importantly, within the context of integrating earth, man and the cosmos. We must learn to be in harmony with the earth, the whole of nature and the elements, with God and the cosmos. Then we shall be truly at peace with ourselves.

To balance these fields, we stand behind the person, and, with our hands, feel and link into the gravity field at about the level of the hips, and having made contact, gradually raise our hands lifting the gravity field as we do. We lift it right up, and gently hold it in place above the head, by tying the energy from our two hands together. The movements should always be smooth and gentle, as we are dealing with very sensitive energies, which are a very real part of the person themselves. Usually one or two movements are sufficient for the field to be lifted into place. When working with the gravity field, a sense of heaviness or weight may often be experienced. This heaviness can be the result of conditions at a physical, mental, emotional or even spiritual level. The old saying that 'that person carries the weight of the world on their shoulders' is literally true. They are weighed down with their cares and responsibilities – it can be felt. Sometimes a very real sense of exertion is required in order to raise the field. Or, the field may be found to be off to one side, or perhaps twisted, if there should be some mis-alignment or deformity in the body structure.

Having brought the gravity field back into place, we can now turn our attention to the magnetic field. Again, stand-ing behind the patient we feel with our hands for the field about 2–3 feet above the head. When we have made contact, we gently bring our hands down and feel a slight pressure, or springiness, against our hands as we do so. We bring this energy down very gently to about 4–5 inches above the head as though we were putting on a beautiful head-dress. Never work quickly, or with a bouncing movement, as this will be felt by the person as an unpleasant jolt. Upon completion of the treatment, always finish with a short blessing for the person's well-being, asking that they might receive healing and protection.

The result of harmonising and integrating these two fields can have very powerful effects, and touch levels which are not easily reached by other means. Once, when we were staying with friends, they arranged for a young girl to come to see us as she kept losing her sight. From time to time, and without warning, she would suddenly go blind, at school or home or anywhere. She had attended doctors and eye spec-ialists, but nothing optically or medically could be found wrong, and they had not been able to help. As we worked with this young girl, we felt that she was co-operating exceptionally well, and there was a good rapport and response. Following the treatment she had no further trouble. Afterwards we were told that her parents had not been getting along very well together when her mother had been pregnant with her, and that they had discussed the matter of separating. In the event, they did not, and had patched up their differences and had remained as a family. But the emotion and trauma, whilst the child was in the womb, had affected her deeply, so that whenever a situation in life arose that was distressing or unpleasant, she just could not bring herself to look at it – she did not want to see it, and so her sight left her.

The healing that took place was at a soul level. When in the womb, an infant is very susceptible to outside atmospheres and tensions. These can affect the child deeply and leave a permanent mark or scar upon their consciousness, sometimes causing a reaction later in life, that the person does not understand. It is for this reason that a pregnant woman should be surrounded with as much love, care and beauty as possible, so that the infant may be enfolded with these qualities. We have also found that these magnetic treatments have been marvellously successful in overcoming morning sickness.

When working with these fields, sometimes visual concepts, symbols or thoughts will arise naturally within the consciousness without having been called forth in any way. When this happens it is important to pass them on to the person concerned. They may have a special meaning for that person. Afterwards, these symbols can become useful visualisation tools when treating other people by choosing whatever one may seem to be appropriate for the moment, and holding the relevant picture clearly in mind.

On one occasion, when working on the heart centre of someone, the picture of a dove came into my thought, and it seemed particularly apt for the person. The dove is, of course, a symbol of peace, and we relate that to the heart centre, but it is also a symbol of the descent of the spirit into matter – a marrying of the two principles. And the heart is a bi-dimensional organ functioning at a physical and spiritual level. So it was, and is, a nice symbol to use.

Another time, I found myself thinking strongly of three particular angels, and when completing the treatment with a final blessing, felt impressed to tell the person of the nearness of the angel kingdom, and always to call upon them for help and comfort in time of need or in any situation of danger or anxiety. She said to me afterwards, 'it's strange you should mention the angels because I felt very strongly today three presences standing around us as we worked'.

Sometimes, as the gravity field is raised to the level of the head, I visualise a golden salver in my hands with all the cares and fears of the illness or situation upon it and with all those things which are holding the person back, and offer this to Christ – 'come unto Me all ye who are heavy laden', that through His grace and love He might take these conditions from the patient. But only if it seems that the person is willing to let go of all these things. Sometimes they are not yet ready to do so. Healing of the consciousness is needed before they reach this state. Occasionally, a silver salver seems, for some reason, to be more appropriate perhaps because those things which are holding the person back are of a more lunar or feminine nature.

Symbols lodging within the consciousness can have a very powerful effect, and it is for this reason that we feel all those which are uplifting, creative and of a spiritual kind are the best. Some visualisation techniques teach the use of fighting, aggressive or destructive symbolism, in overcoming illness and disease; but we prefer the other approach.

There are, of course, a number of things one can do to help heal oneself if no healer is available. For instance, there are numerous methods of relaxation, meditation and yoga, all of which can bring about a state of harmony and well-being. Such practices, if carried out regularly, help us to cope better with the demands of life in general and enable us to deal effectively and calmly with them without becoming a casualty of them.

Here we give a self-healing exercise which can be carried out for oneself at home, and which will help to harmonise and balance body, mind and soul.

Sit on a chair quietly with feet on the ground. With one hand behind on the base of the spine place the other one over the solar plexus. Gradually one will feel a sensation of warmth, both in the two areas of the body, and in the hands. Wait for a few moments until the warmth or energy in the two hands feels the same. Then, with one hand still on the base of the spine, move the other to a position over the heart. Hold there until the sensation of warmth evens out. Next move the hand which was over the heart up to the thyroid, with the other hand still at the base of the spine and, as before, let the energies balance. Then remove the hand from the back of the spine, and cup it around the nape of the neck, so that we are now balancing the energy of that area, the pituitary, with the thyroid. When this has been done, take the front hand from the thyroid and place it gently over the forehead, with the other hand still over the nape of the neck at the back of the head. Finally, with one hand still over the forehead, place the other hand over or above the crown of the head, and keep them in this position for a few moments.

With this exercise we have now balanced our own chakra centres. To begin, do not stay over long in any one position. After a while, when we have become accustomed to this exercise, we may feel that one particular area of the body may need more attention than others, and we can work on it accordingly. Should we have pain in any part of the body it is comforting to hold a hand over the area, and mentally concentrate on healing being given to it.

Once we have become accustomed to this exercise, balancing our own spiritual/chakra centres in this way can, at the same time, be a very beneficial and pleasant form of meditation and relaxation. If done in a prayerful way, it can be very effective, and help to bring about a real sense of well-being.

10

ABSENT HEALING

If, for one reason or another, it is not possible for a person to visit a healer, it is still possible for them to receive help. There is another source of power available to the healer in the form of absent healing. When we know how, we can direct healing, through prayer and meditation, to another person who is unable to be present, and distance is no obstacle. We can heal at a distance.

In a way, the term absent healing is something of a misnomer, because contact may be made with the person's higher self through prayer and meditation, and the calling of the name. When we speak someone's name, the sound of that name goes forth on the subtle ethers, and makes a connection, at an interdimensional level, with the person concerned. That is why christening is so important, because for the first time that person's note is sounded, and their individuality proclaimed. Their identity is established.

For prayer to be effective we must, first of all, achieve a meditative state, by raising ourselves to a higher level of consciousness. Through our higher self we have contact with the source of all power and with universal consciousness, and meditation places us in a position to make that contact. Prayer and meditation are inseparable, but not interchangeable; prayer cannot take the place of meditation nor can meditation replace prayer. Communication is a two way process, and, whilst prayer is speaking to God, meditation is listening to what He has to say. There is an old Egyptian saying which is perhaps relevant in this regard – 'He who knows how to listen knows how to speak'. We must learn 'to be still and know', and then our prayers truly have power.

It is important, therefore in absent healing, first of all to achieve that level of quiet and stillness by a few minutes of meditation; to take our mind away from worldly matters and raise it up to a spiritual dimension. Then, through prayer, we can ask, in the name of Christ, for healing to be brought to the person concerned. Always we ask for that which is best for each person at the particular time, not what we think is needed. In prayer, we should never outline what we want, but just make the request, and it will be answered according to the need of the person and not necessarily in the way that we might expect. The higher powers know what is best.

We got a telephone call one evening from a young friend, in great distress, because her baby boy of a few months had been rushed into hospital. We were asked to put his name on our prayer list for absent healing and also in the sanctuary, which, of course, we did, asking at the same time that he would receive the help he needed.

Some time later, she kindly wrote to tell us that he had just passed his first birthday and had made a full and unscathed recovery from the meningitis. Apparently he was the wonder of the hospital. She had just been visiting someone and they still remembered him and all the nurses were asking for him. On his first check-up after being discharged, the consultant had said to her that, quite frankly, not only was it marvellous that he had survived, but that he suffered no side effects – 'Someone was praying for this little fellow' were the words he used. So, we have the case where skilled medical treatment with loving nursing and prayer combine to make a truly holistic approach.

Sometimes in our healing treatments, we are inclined to underestimate the power of prayer. Too much emphasis, perhaps, is placed upon the technique, upon doing something, instead of adapting a more relaxed attitude, and linking in consciously to another level of knowledge and power. The technique is important, but it is what happens within, and through the techniques, that determines the level of being which is touched, whether at a purely physical level or at some higher state of consciousness. This is the part played by prayer.

One morning, the telephone rang and a woman asked if our healing group gave any healing for animals, as her dog had received an injury to its back, and it was being brought to the vet. I replied that I regretted we did not but said I would try and contact someone who might be able to help even though the person was not a healer. Then, in that strange way that events sometimes happen, the telephone rang in the late afternoon. This time it was the voice of a young girl, obviously filled with concern, who said that her cat, Luigi, was very ill and with the vet who said he did not think that it would live through the night. She said her mother had just met a friend who knew us, and suggested they ask if we could say a prayer for the cat – she pleaded, would I please say a prayer for her cat? Just to say a prayer – that, surely, was not asking too much. So I said I would that evening, and asked her to let me know how the cat got on. I was glad I did that, because I had forgotten to ask her telephone number, or address and did not even know who the mutual friend was. How strange I thought to myself – a request for two animals in the one day was most unusual; and I wondered about the dog.

Later that evening I was writing, with one eye on the clock, as there was a television programme coming up that I wanted to watch. Suddenly, I felt an insistent inner prompting, 'What about that little cat? In pain, gasping for breath, miserable. Are you just going to sit there whilst it suffers and struggles for life? Are you going to leave it any longer before doing something? And what about that little girl who is worrying so much? Are you going to let her down?' And so, I just had to stop what I was doing and go into our little sanctuary to meditate and pray. After a while, I felt that I had made a good contact with an unknown cat in an unknown place, and had a certain sense of inner calm and assurance that was good. I got up feeling uplifted and lighter in spirit, and glad that I had made the effort.

The next day my young friend rang to tell me that the cat was better and was coming home the following day. The

vet had phoned to say that the cat had taken some break-
fast, and was now curled up comfortably and fast asleep. He
had not expected it to survive the night and did not know
what had happened. Subsequent x-rays showed that its
lungs were clear. So, Luigi, the cat, impressed a lesson, once
again, that there is always something we can do, even if it is
only to 'say a prayer'. We must always remember that if we
wish to be of service, we may be asked to be the answer to
someone else's prayer. We must always hold ourselves
ready to answer that call.

If we could obtain all our needs, by our own effort, we
would have no necessity of prayer. We resort to prayer
when the requirements are beyond our own capability. In
such a case, we acknowledge the existence of a source of
power and intelligence that is superior to our own resources.
When we take it upon ourselves to be a channel of help and
healing for others, we stand in a position between the source
of supply and the seeker of that help. Once we have com-
mitted ourselves, through prayer and dedication, to be of
service, we create a link which is ever open with that divine
source of supply.

Someone has only to ask of us, and a direct connection is
instantly made. It is like a radio set which is tuned to a
specific frequency and left permanently turned on. It becomes alive as soon as the transmitting station starts broad-
casting. At other times it is silent. We have often found that
someone has asked to have their name, or that of a friend or
relative, included in our absent healing list, or for help at
some other level, only to have them ring up shortly afterwards to say that there has been an improvement in the
condition, or that the prayer was answered before it was
possible for us to put the request into action at a physical
level. It is important, then, always to hold ourselves ready,
and as soon as any request is made, consciously to link ourselves mentally with the source, even if only for a few
moments. For it is the quality of the connection that is made
that is important, and not the duration, and also the faith

and love with which it is made.

When people come together in a group, they form a more powerful channel for help and healing to be brought to others. In group work it is especially important not to mention what is wrong with the person, as this only places a mental picture in the minds of others. A visual image can become a very powerful force, if concentrated upon continually, and can actually impede the healing process. Also, we are very careful not to trespass upon another person's privacy and only put names on our absent healing list when requested by the person themselves, or by a close friend or relative on their behalf. Apart from the question of imposing upon another person's life, absent healing is much more effective when the patient concerned co-operates, by attuning mentally at the appropriate time, and this has been demonstrated many times. A typical case was where there was someone on our list for many weeks, at the request of a friend, but with the person's knowledge and consent. The person, however, never linked with us at the regular time until one evening she decided that she would. That night, for the first time in many months, she was completely free from pain.

If we should ever feel like sending help to someone without their knowledge or request, we can always ask and visualise that they might be surrounded by the light and consciousness of Christ, and be guided by the Holy Spirit – that, and no more. In due course of time, an inner change or outlook may be brought about voluntarily.

One time, a member of our absent healing group which is called 'The Circle of Light' put the name of a friend of his on our absent healing list. This friend had recently had a serious accident, which left him partially paralysed. At the time, he was in a remedial clinic, and feeling very depressed. One day, he asked for his friend to come and see him, and told him that he had been contemplating taking his own life when, one evening, he felt impressed upon to pray, although he was not in the habit of doing this. Whilst he was praying, he fell asleep and had a dream in which he saw, and recognised, his friend amongst a group of people gathered in a circle. He also saw the leader of the group and described this person in great detail. In the dream the group was surrounded by an intensely bright light. In due course, he received a healing of the injury to his spine, to the amazement of the doctors, who had expected him to be confined to a wheelchair for the rest of his life. So, we see how the strength and dedication of a group can help to bring about a miracle in a person's life.

In group absent healing, it is very important to meet on a regular basis and at a regular time. All things are cyclical in nature, and when we meet consistently, and regularly, we set up an energy pattern or frequency that is known, and has its reflection in the divine world. If we solicit help from that level, it is incumbent upon us to keep our appointments conscientiously with regard to time. In all of this we must not forget, or underestimate the part played by the angels of healing. They can use what we have to offer during our periods of quiet contemplation and prayer, in ways we may not fully understand, and perhaps more than we can imagine.

In addition to our group work, names are placed in the colour-light sanctuary in our home, which radiates its peaceful and healing atmosphere day and night. The light never goes out, and the colours are changed regularly throughout the day. Our interest in maintaining an ever-burning light or lamp arose through coming in touch with the Lamplighter Movement which was founded by W. Tudor Pole, a truly remarkable person. In 1940, during those dark days of the Second World War, at his suggestion, and with the encouragement of King George VI and many leaders of church and state, the striking of Big Ben in London at 9 pm was broadcast by the BBC over its world-wide network. The 'Silent Minute', as it was called whilst the chimes rang out, became a focus of unity and common accord in a prayer for peace. In many oppressed countries in Europe, in prisoner of war camps and elsewhere the sound of Big Ben struck a chord of hope in the hearts of those who heard it, and kept aflame a glimmer of light in the souls of those who held a vision where all people would be free and at peace with one another.

When, in 1964, the striking of Big Ben at 9 pm was discontinued by the BBC, Tudor Pole received instruction from a high spiritual source, that light should replace sound, and so the Lamplighter Movement was born. It was requested that ever-burning lamps should be lit in homes and sanctuaries, with a simple service of dedication as a sign that here were houses from which prayer and meditation were rising. This was to be seen as an outer symbol of inner intent, and a declaration of the reality of the spiritual world. Such lights kindle their own counterparts in the spiritual realm, and can be seen as a sign of an awakening to the light, and faith in the future that people everywhere may live together in peace, harmony and in a spirit of brotherly love and friendly co-operation. It is for this reason that we recommend that an ever-burning lamp should be kept within every home and sanctuary.

In other times, people made a clear distinction between visible light and spiritual light, and in the Bulgarian language, for instance, there are two words for light. *Svetlina* is used for visible light, or physical light, whilst the word *Videlina* is reserved for invisible or spiritual light. Thus, an ever-burning lamp that has been dedicated to the light, establishes a means of communication, for the inflow of spiritual power and protection, from the divine world to us. To have lived once within the healing presence of living light is an experience not lightly put aside.

'May peace be with your coming and Peace be on your going.
May the light enfold you'.

11

PASSING OVER

It so happens from time to time that health is not brought about, that someone is not healed – and we are asked why?

Not every person gets well. No doctor cures all patients. No healer restores all people to health. In the ways of the world and life we all have a time to come and a time to go, and the manner and moment of our passing is not in our hands but in accordance with some purpose beyond our control. We must realise this and not look upon some terminal outcome as a failure but rather the natural time for that person to pass. If we can sense this impending condition when working with someone then we can often turn this period of time into an opportunity for growth and acceptance. A time of grace for the person where much inner and outer work may be done, and where the quality of life for a while may be improved so that eventually they pass in peace. Sometimes a person may seem to have received a healing only to have a relapse after a while. It seems for a time as though they have had a remission but this, if used wisely, can be a period of grace.

Most people when they are approaching the end of their time know but are reluctant to broach the subject. And most relatives and friends are afraid to raise the matter for fear of causing anxiety to the person concerned. But more often than not they are only too glad to talk about this in an atmosphere of loving kindness, understanding and support. At first a person may find it easier to talk to a comparative stranger rather than to someone close to them, and this is where a healer or counsellor can play a very important part. In today's world most doctors just do not have the time to spend in this way, not that they are in anyway insensitive to the need. This is where we have found that skilled and knowledgeable counselling combined with spiritual healing can provide a very good support to orthodox medical treatment.

In severe cases such as cancer, where the treatment is exceptionally invasive and disturbing to the body we have often been told by patients that without this back up it would never have been possible for them to have withstood the side effects of the treatment. Frequently we have found that the level of pain has been considerably lessened or eliminated, and consequently the need of medication reduced.

This period of communication with a patient often provides the space which the person needs to come to terms with unexpressed fears, to talk about and release resentments, to sort out and even mend relationships and friendships. And perhaps most important of all to be actually able to speak with those who are their nearest and dearest, and tell them them things they have always wanted to say, but never did. For those around them this will require a gentle understanding and patience and an ability to respond in an appropriate way.

We have often seen during such a time a complete inner transformation take place in people, a virtual change in character. From being aggressive or resentful they have become caring, gentle, considerate and even interested in the circumstances of others. It is important to realise that we must not 'carry over' with us a lot of unfinished business as this will only hold us back when we pass. The residue will still reside in our consciousness and somehow in some way we will have to resolve and heal these issues. It is much easier to do so while we can when we are alive, and we should not neglect the opportunity. We are not suddenly different people when we 'wake-up' on the other side.

However, healing also takes place on the 'other side' for the angels of healing are as active there as they are here. If we can deal with most of our problems and difficulties here and now then we pass over a stronger and freer person and the transition into the next world will be that much easier. For life is continuous. Death is not the end, only another beginning. Death is not something to be feared.

Death has become the most ill described word in the human language. It conjures up thoughts of darkness, despair and desolation. It inculcates feelings of fear – fear of the unknown and fear of exchanging irrevocably the familiar pattern of existence for the untried and mistrusted world of oblivion. In ignorance all manner of conditions have been ascribed to that which has been called the hereafter so that superstition and confusion abound.

From the first moment of our arrival in this world we lose all knowledge of the manner and choosing and time of our so-called birth. From this moment on there is only one thing of which we can be certain, in the whole of our sojourn upon this plane and it is that we must surely die. All else will be subject to circumstance and change. How strange, therefore, that this only certain fact should be so misunderstood and so little studied. Strange also, is it not, that we must always speak about being 'born into the world'. Within us we know that 'we are not of this world' and that we have come from somewhere. It is to this place that we must one day return.

In like manner, we have become confused in our understanding of the words *life* and *death*. Death is that point of transition between one state of consciousness and another – nothing more. It has no existence or duration. It is not a state of being. It signifies change no more no less. We are familiar with the movement of the hands of a clock as they approach the changing of an hour. As the last few seconds are ticked away the minute hand, the arbiter of the hours, moves inexorably out of the shades of the dying hour into the dawn of the new one just born. At one precise instant the transition takes place. The ending of one hour is the beginning of the next. There is no interval between the two. Birth and death are synonymous and instantaneous.

In our work with the dying we must try and help them

to understand that passing is not the end and that they can look forward to meeting again those loved ones who have passed ahead of them. And in turn they can look forward to a reunion, at some time in the future with those dear ones they are leaving behind. Those who have returned from 'near death' experiences have amply confirmed the reality of 'another place'. They speak of beautiful surroundings full of light and colour and even of meeting people they once knew. Most people describe the experience as so beautiful that they did not wish to come back and would have gladly remained where they were.

After working with people in this way we have found that much may be accomplished and at this point they are in a state of peace with themselves and with their relationship to the world and others. As one person said to us '... I am ready now to go, or to stay'.

Once a person has passed over we must continue to try and do our best to help them forward and not hold them back. We do much to hold a person back by grieving un-necessarily. Grief acts as a kind of bond, an attachment, whereas thoughts of love and joy will do much to release them. We can do much to help a loved one in their new state of consciousness by asking in our prayers that they may be surrounded with the light and protection of Christ, and guided in the pathways of truth.

That we can help those who have gone on was brought home to me after that experience in Greece of watching the sunset. As I walked back to the hotel there was a little stone church on the way with a simple wooden bench outside covered by an awning of branches to provide some shade in the hot noon day sun. I stopped and sat on the bench in the growing dusk to think about things and after a while wondered if the little church would be open, thinking it would be nice to go inside for a few minutes. I got up and found that the handle turned beneath my hand, so I gently pushed the door open. It was completely dark inside and I could see nothing as I stood there in the entrance. Almost immediately I felt a presence behind me and, slightly start-led, looked over my right shoulder but there was no one there, and then over my left shoulder, but no one there either. Then it seemed that I was in the middle of a throng of people all crowding past me to get into the little church as though they had been waiting for it to be opened.

So I slowly and carefully groped my way forward until I reached the first pew. Kneeling there I asked that the light of Christ would fill with love and peace and protection, this place and all those who entered in. And I also asked that all those who were here now in the 'in between', which is just a breath away, would be led to that place or realm of exper-ience which was right for them at this time. That the light would always guide them safely along the pathways of truth and that they would never walk in the dark, but always seek the light, that they should find their home in the land of light. Sending them a blessing and a thought of love that they might go their way in peace, I opened my eyes. It was as though the little church was filled with light for I could clearly see every detail and corner — and I went out into the evening closing the door softly behind me.

This experience impressed upon me that we must not forget those who have 'gone on'. We can still help, through our prayers and meditation, our loved ones and others also who have passed over to the other side.

    'Will you ferry me over the river?' I said to the man who stood on the bank.

    'I could,' the Boatman replied, 'but are you willing to pay the price? Many there are who come but few who make the crossing. The river is wide, the rocks are sharp, the current swift and deceitful and there is no turning back once a beginning has been made. Only disaster, or the far bank await those who make the attempt.'

    'The price is high but the reward is great,' I replied. 'To serve is both the price and reward – there is no higher. I am willing to pay the price.'

    'Mostly,' continued the Boatman, 'they come and stand

awhile and look and ponder, and then sadly retrace their steps once more. The ties of earth are strong, the pull of spirit weak. Desire it is, or fear or bitterness which pulls them back.'

'All these have I overcome,' I said, 'no longer do I desire the pleasures of worldly things, nor yet spurn or scorn their rightful use and place in the affairs of men. Bitterness is foreign to me and I can see that one who approaches here with such a feeling will find the outlook to be sterner still than that which he has left behind, and will turn back with heavy heart to learn the lesson over once again. And fear I have conquered also for I have learnt that out of humility grows trust, and where trust is fear is not.'

'Well have you spoken,' he replied, 'but is your trust well placed — in what do you trust?'

'Is not the password trust?' I said. 'My trust is in Him. If I will be His servant He will not see me led astray or let my feet be dashed against the rocks.'

'Rightly have you said that trust is the password, and trust is mutual,' he replied. 'So that you may know that this is so I will guide you across if you will take the oar — what say you friend? The choice is yours.'

'If you are willing I am ready,' I replied, and as the boat slipped from the bank the waters instantly became a river of flowing light and the rocks as flashing jewels. The sky was filled with exquisite colours, quite inconceivable to mortal eyes and from the far bank glorious sounds of heavenly music rose. I turned to my boatman, to find him transformed into a shining figure of shimmering light — and we were at the other bank.

12

CONTINUITY OF CONSCIOUSNESS

There is a growing awareness amongst some people that we have lived before, that perhaps this is not our first sojourn on the earth. Many eastern religions adhere to the doctrine of reincarnation, so that already a large number of the world's population incline to that view. Today we find that many young children naturally refer to the fact that they remember having lived before, or refer to the fact that they knew their brother or sister or parents, when they were together at some previous time. But, unfortunately, their memories are dimmed by the teaching and consciousness of the outside world, and also because of superstition and fear of being ridiculed, many parents correct their children for having such fanciful ideas. Notwithstanding all the good that it does, education also does much to stamp upon us some false ideas and dogmas for a large part of our life, so that afterwards when we come in contact with esoteric thinking and other unorthodox views we have to go through the difficult process of unlearning a lot of what we were taught before we can come to accept such concepts.

It is natural to look for proof of things but the fact that a certain premise can neither be proved nor disproved is no valid reason for rejecting it entirely. Better by far to place it for the time being on the mantelpiece of our mind – neither to reject or accept it – but to hold it in the background of our consciousness until such time as our own inner feelings decide one way or the other. Sometimes we have experiences out of the ordinary which do not appear to conform to normally accepted patterns of reality. But, even if we cannot explain them fully we can not deny them and must give them recognition.

One evening when I got home from work Elizabeth called to me as I came into the hall, 'There's a letter there for you from Mary!' Mary was the healer in Wales with whom we had become good friends after that first meeting when she had given me a healing. I opened the letter and as I read it noticed it was just 7 pm, the time that Mary would meditate for fifteen minutes to send out absent healing to her patients. Thinking that it would be nice to join with her in thought and prayer I went straight into the study and sat down, still holding her letter in my hand as I did so. Becoming quiet and reaching upward and outward I soon felt that I had made a very good contact with her in her healing meditation.

Suddenly I felt myself travelling back a long way in time to find that we were standing on the shore of a curving bay looking out over the water which was sparkling in the sunlight. We were both dressed in long white robes and I knew that it was somewhere on the American continent and that we were facing west. I felt slightly puzzled because I knew instinctively that it was not the Pacific that we were looking at, and that there was land ahead of me and land behind me. Then, as has sometimes been the case in such circumstances, information was given in a series of phrases, very concisely and very precisely and it came like this:

> *South America.*
> *Bolivia.*
> *Indians.*
> *Before Columbus.*
> *You learnt that there.*

With that, the scene faded and I found myself sitting in the study once more.

As I did not really know where Bolivia was except that it was somewhere in South America I reached for an atlas but, in a feeling of frustration, put it back on the shelf again without even opening it because it was not a very good one and I did not think that it would help me greatly. Then I remembered that some time before the *National Geographic* magazine had had a map of South America. Now, there were copies on the shelves and others stacked in bundles on the floor in absolutely no order. I put my hand down and picked up a copy at random and that very one which was then two years old had this map of South America. Opening the map I found what I was meant to find, that Bolivia was a landlocked country with a great lake or inland sea – Lake Titicaca – which, with the Andes Mountains, separates it from Peru. Thus it was that we must have been standing on the shores of Lake Titicaca. On turning the map over, the other side had a series of smaller maps relating to the historical periods of America. The first one was headed pre-Columbian and mentioned that there was a very advanced ancient civilisation there on the shores of the lake, the great Mayan Indian people. Also the Andes is believed to have been the home of one of the mystery schools of olden times.

When one has experiences such as this it is not possible to deny or disregard them. We cannot just push them out of our consciousness. We must give them recognition. Just as sometimes we may be granted glimpses of the past at other times we may be allowed to catch a vision of the future.

Now, weddings are not one of my favourite social events and when our nephew in South Africa wrote to say that he was engaged it did not cause undue concern because it was obviously out of the question to make such a trip. However, when some time later we heard that he and his bride-to-be had decided to get married in the Isle of Wight where her parents lived, and we received an invitation to the wedding, I immediately tried to think up all sorts of excuses why I could not go, such as being too busy, although this would have been most unpopular with Elizabeth.

Then one night about two months before the date of the

wedding I awoke in full consciousness to find myself walking down a little flint pebble path, with Elizabeth by my
side, towards a quaint, very old small church which, most
unusually, had its entrance at the side. The path was separated from the road by a green grass sward and other people
were getting out of cars and walking towards the church.
Some were dressed very formally and many of the younger
people very casually and colourfully. As we approached the
entrance we were met by a rather rotund, jovial looking
minister who greeted us warmly and he himself took us
down the aisle and showed us into our places about four
pews from the front on the right hand side. With that the
vision ended; and I felt that, in a way, my fate had been
sealed. For a while it was quite difficult to live with that
experience for in some strange way I felt that I could exert
my free will at any time and make a positive decision not to
go. There was nothing seemingly to stop me from doing so.
Yet, I felt inwardly that it would be wrong to make such a
choice and was ill at ease about such a decision.

So eventually we went and as we had never been to the
Isle of Wight before we looked forward to going somewhere
new and Elizabeth was pleased to be with her family. Naturally, I was interested to see how events would turn out. We
booked into our hotel and later that evening Elizabeth's
brother came into our room to say that he had just been to
look at the church where the service was to be held. He said:
'It's the quaintest little church – it's tiny!', and so I wondered. The next day events turned out exactly as I had fore-
seen them, the flint path, the green grass on one side, people
in different types of dress, the jovial rotund rector who
greeted us warmly and showed us to our places on the right
hand side four pews from the front. And, of course, the little
church with it's entrance at the side.

When one has a precognitive vision which later comes to
pass in exact detail it not only confirms the reality of that
experience but also confirms, or at least lends weight to, the

validity of an experience of some event which took place long ago at some other time. In the experiencing of such happenings it is known in full consciousness that one is travelling either forwards or backwards in time. It is quite clear, there is no doubt. But it also forces one to have a different concept of time and consciousness than that normally held. That time, perhaps, is not as fixed as we might think and that in some way there is a 'free area' around every event wherein we can exercise our free will. In this way we become either in or out of step with the flow of the tide of time and events.

One of the most powerful optical instruments in use today is the 200–inch telescope on Mount Palomar in California. It can reach out into space to a distance of 2,000 million light years to the galaxy clusters in Hydra, amongst the most distant objects yet discerned. This means that it can detect an object which is so far distant that the light emitted by it and travelling at a speed of 186,000 miles per second has taken 2,000 million years to reach us. In other words, we observe it today as it was 2,000 million years ago. The position it occupies in space today is greatly different to that in which we see it because of the recession of the galaxies within the expanding universe.

We are withdrawing from the Hydra cluster at a rate equivalent to about one fifth of the speed of light and this borders the limit of our observable horizon at present. Radio telescopes can see still further into space, and with advances in technology we will soon have instruments in space which will greatly extend our vision. The ultimate horizon of visibility, however, extends out into space where galaxies are receding from us at a speed equal to the speed of light. Beyond that we become invisible to each other for the light that is emitted can never reach us.

It is equally true that light from our own galaxy is also travelling out through space so that an observer on a planet in a distant galaxy situated on our horizon, and equipped with a similar telescope to our 200 inch, would see our system as it was 2,000 million years ago. From examination of the rocks of our own earth, radio carbon dating gives us a time interval of approximately 1,800 million years since the cooling down of its surface. If we suppose that our hypothetical observer possesses super-powerful instruments he will be able to observe the cooling down of our planet and our birth upon it – if he waits long enough! To him the condensation of our earth and our arising upon it are events of the future. In round figures, what 'is' today for us 'will be' for our distant friend 2,000 million years hence, or to put it another way, what 'is' for him 'was' for us aeons ago.

It is easy to see that that great distance of space which separates us contains a true, permanent record of events concerning our planet from its birth to the present day. Every interval or stage along the endless path represents a particular age in the process of evolution of our world, an historical register of some event in our worldly civilisation. In measure of linear distance a point midway between the two galaxies contains a message from our past dispatched 1,000 million years ago. Speeding towards its destination it passes another on the way due to be received by us in a similar period of time from now. Thus the scale of that distance may be constructed in terms of the past or future depending on our point of view. In the same way that we can focus our terrestrial telescope upon near objects or those which lie at the limit of its range it seems not improbable that we will eventually be able to develop highly sensitive instruments capable of focusing on the vibrational activity in space. Perhaps our faraway friend already possesses such an instrument and can 'tune-in' at will to any period of our history.

If, for instance, we look out of the window of a high-rise building into the street below and watch the passers-by coming and going we can, if we wish, focus our attention on one particular person and follow their every movement as they go about their business; a silent, invisible observer. In the same way a satellite orbiting high above the earth can photograph the scene below. By enlargement, a particular street, building or person may be singled out for inspection – and so on to infinity. The impression of that scene or person's reality has been transmitted inexorably out into the depths of space, travelling relentlessly onward into eternity. The moment has been captured forever. And so it is for every other point upon the earth's surface as though our planet was, in effect, a giant projector, with interstellar space its screen.

It is not difficult, therefore, to envisage a series of concentric shells representing contours of consciousness, as it were, or specific moments of history, events of the past surrounding our earth. Each shell denotes a certain time in the record of the earth and any point on that shell is of the same instant of time as every other point upon it.

There is, of course, no interval between the contours, just a steady continuous flow of expression. However, if the past can be represented by a series of concentric expanding shells the future can be represented by a similar series contracting towards the hub or source of all creation and expression. The particular shell which we occupy at this time is for us the present, but, just where in the great plan this shell lies we do not know.

We know that there are people who can foresee the future, prophets who can accurately foretell events yet to come. These people have, apparently, the ability to 'tune in' with their consciousness to one of the inner contours. There are others who have been able to describe in detail happenings of the past. It seems that they must have 'tuned in' to one of the outer contours.

Such people as these are able to transfer their consciousness radially with respect to the flow of time. Yet others have been witness to some distant event taking place remote from them. They have merely transferred their consciousness circumferentially to another point upon the contour of the present. Thus we can see that past, present and future exist together and are but different facets or extensions of consciousness.

Returning to the analogy of the projector, let us, if we can, imagine a spherical projector using spherical film, the the film represents the great plan or thought. The film is illuminated by the light of life and consciousness which has its source in the projector or creator, and the picture thrown on the screen represents our physical existence.

The analogy is, however, too simple for it precludes the existence of free will. How can this quality be made to fit into our scheme of things? Let us examine this film a little more closely, for therein lies the possibility of choice. This is no ordinary film, comprising a series of views and scenes with the various actors and actresses playing their parts strictly in accordance with the dictates of the author. In such the story is rigid and allows but little interpretation, and that only by the director. By the time the story gets to the players the only interpretation left to them is nothing more than expression. But in our spherical film, things are different.

Here the story or great plan is entirely symbolical. The various scenes are composed of cosmic urges and influences, symbols which, upon being illuminated by the light of life and consciousness, allow interpretation. The interpretation of these symbols and urges by consciousness as it flows through them produces the circumstances and pattern of life, events of physical manifestation and life as we live it. The more accurate the interpretation the more closely do we follow God's will and desire and the more smoothly flows the process of living. To interpret them inaccurately or to contort them to suit our personal desires is to go against the will of God. Life will then be full of difficulties and a burden instead of a joy. Worse still, we will lose the continuity of the story or great plan so that we shall find it increasingly difficult to follow and understand as it gradually unfolds. Only when our interpretation is perfect in every detail and all our desires identical with those of the Author, will we have attained complete attunement with the cosmic and become that which was intended – a true companion of our creator.

All is written in the book of life. Our own record is imprinted indelibly on a page of the universe. Whether that which will be revealed is pleasing or otherwise depends upon ourselves here, now! Each of us, is our own recording angel, and collectively that of planet earth.

We are all subject to the law of cause and effect and through the expression of our gift of free will create for ourselves a future that is in line with the divine plan, the purpose of our lives, or a future the consequences of which may not have been intended and which may bring us added burdens with which to deal. We all come into incarnation with certain work to do, certain responsibilities and certain relationships to come to terms with or enjoy. To learn and grow through the lessons that life can teach us, we must try to cultivate a sense of awareness and intuition to discriminate and make wise decisions and choices.

Every moment of each day we are constantly making decisions and taking actions, which, no matter how small, bring in their train certain results or conditions. These results or conditions produce of themselves circumstances which in turn require us to act or decide in a certain way. Thus, we are continuously weaving a pattern of the future which we may find pleasing or otherwise. From time to time in our lives, greater issues arise and after due deliberation we make a choice or decision which charts the way ahead in a major way until another such event arrives on the scene. These turning points in our lives may be either opportunities to be grasped or experiences through which we have to pass and live for one reason or another. The ability to appreciate the full value and meaning of such moments depends upon the degree of our awareness and understanding of the forces which lie beneath and mould our lives, for the actions of one life influence the pattern of the next. We reap the karma we sow whether for better or for worse.

We are accustomed in our examination of phenomena to employ a process of reasoning so that we may learn something of their nature and obtain an understanding of the occurrence. We can reason either inductively or deductively, or perhaps employ both methods depending upon the circumstances. When we reason deductively, we are looking for a logical or likely outcome as a result of a certain action. Deductive reasoning is looking forward from a known cause to a possible effect. On the other hand inductive reasoning is searching backwards to the origin of something from a known result. Inductive reasoning looks backwards from a known effect to a possible cause. It can be seen that the phenomenon or event may at the same time be both cause and effect in a series of interconnected happenings. The effect of a prior cause in turn becomes the cause of some succeeding event.

This can well be illustrated by the swing of a pendulum. If we imagine a pendulum swinging, it describes an arc, one half of which we can term cause, and the other half, effect. At the midpoint of the swing, at that one instant, cause and effect are synonymous – one and the same. On its return swing, like the alternating current of electricity, cause and effect change over, but still the mid-point remains unchanged, being both at that one precise moment.

From an esoteric point of view, this analogy can be used to illustrate and explain many things. We can apply the pendulum to creation where it swings from the un-manifest through the manifest on into its shadow. From the thought through the moment to its memory, and from the idea to the reality and on to the illusion. From the future to the present and into the past. In our consideration of time, we are apt to think of ourselves as rushing headlong into the future, and leaving the past behind. The present is both the future and the past. The future has already happened, the past is not dead. It would be easier if we were to conceive that the future approaches us rather than the other way round. We can then see that if we can raise our sensitivity, increase our awareness to forces which are already in existence, then we will be in a better position to take any necessary action and prepare ourselves for whatever may be in our path, to be in a state of readiness to avail of some opportunity that comes our way – so that we recognise it before it is too late – has passed by.

Thus, it can be seen that the closer we can live to the midpoint of the pendulum's swing, the closer we are to that point of balance, of attunement with the creative forces. We live in a shadow world, but the more closely we can approach that point of equipoise, of serenity, the nearer will we be able to manifest the divine ideas which continuously flow through us and more perfectly bring about God's plan in a veritable world of Light. When one day we are able to stand, in a planetary sense, upon the threshold of the gateway of creation, no more shall we be subject to life or death as we know them. Eternal. But ever higher in the evolutionary scale stand those true cosmic beings, the lords of light, those great luminous ones. Unchanging, forever changeless. They who maintain the eternal swing of the universe and chart and control its course.

> ... and so swings the cosmic pendulum of life and light from out of the mists of the dawn of time through the glory of the eternal noon-day sun on into the shades of the sunset of eternity, until once more the roles are reversed and a new heaven and a new earth are born out of the depths of the old – moved by the breath of God ...

Body-Mind Meditation
A Gateway to Spirituality

Louis Hughes, OP

You can take this book as your guide for a fascinating journey that need not take you beyond your own hall door. For it is an in-ward journey, and it will take you no further than God who, for those who want him as a friend, lives within. On the way to God-awareness, you will be invited to experience deep relaxation of body and mind.

Body-Mind Meditation can help you become a more integrated balanced person. It is an especially helpful approach to meditation if the pace of life is too fast for you, or if you find yourself frequently tense or exhausted.

SPIRITUALITY
AND
HOLISTIC LIVING

Sr. Theresa Feist

You are in search of wholeness. You have a body, mind and spiritual life. Your spirit cannot soar if your feet are heavy. Your mind is confused when your blood is stagnant. You need to care properly for your temple.

AN EASY GUIDE
TO
MEDITATION

Roy Eugene Davis

Meditation is the natural process to use to release tension, reduce stress, increase awareness, concentrate more effectively and be open to life. In this book you will learn how to meditate correctly for inner growth and spiritual awareness. Specific guidelines are provided to assist the beginner as well as the more advanced meditator. Here are proven techniques used by accomplished meditators for years: *prayer, mantra, sound–light contemplation, ways to expand consciousness and to experience transcendence.*

Benefits of correct meditation practice include: deep relaxation, stress reduction, inner calm, improved powers of intelligence, and strengthening of the immune system. People in all walks of life can find here the keys to living life as it was meant to be lived.

An Easy Guide to Meditation was written by one who knows how to meditate and who, for decades, has been teaching the process to thousands of people all over the world. Roy Eugene Davis has written many other books including *Our Awakening World, Secrets of Inner Power, With God We Can* and *God Has Given Us Every Good Thing.*

Over 100,000 copies sold.

THE PURSUIT
OF
MEANING

Joseph Fabry

The Pursuit of Meaning is written for the millions of people who are healthy but believe they are sick, because they feel empty; for those who are looking for meaning in frantic activity, in money, power, excitement, sex, alcohol, drugs; for those who are looking for meaning in laws and rules and dogmas rather than searching for it personally. Every mature person has been expelled from his own paradise and lived through his own concentration camp. To help man endure this has always been the tasks of prophets, priests, philosophers and educators. Now they are joined by the psychologists. Logotheraphy supplies one contemporary answer to man's age-old problem of how to live after the expulsion and how to find meaning during and after the trials of suffering.

THE POWER OF CHARISMATIC HEALING

Andy O'Neill

The Power of Charismatic Healing deals specifically with healing by the laying on of hands. It is the story of Andy O'Neill's personal experience of healing in this manner.

The Power of Charismatic Healing will challenge a whole host of non-believers with its rational business-like approach. It was not written by a mystic or a priest but by a businessman who lives in and enjoys today's world.

CHARISMATIC HEALING IN THE MODERN WORLD

Andy O'Neill

Athetists, agnostics and people of other beliefs may question or reject the basis of the Charismatic Renewal Movement and its Healing Ministry – the Christian faith – but the happenings described in this book, which range from the simple to the incredible, cannot be denied.

An introduction to
IRISH HIGH CROSSES

Hilary Richardson & John Scarry

The Irish high crosses are the most original and interesting of all the monuments which stud the Irish landscape. They are of international importance in early medieval art. For their period there is little to equal them in the sculpture of western Europe as a whole.

This beautiful book gives basic information about the crosses. A general survey is followed by an inventory to accompany the large collection of photographs which illustrate their variety and richness. In this way readers will readily have at their disposal an extensive range of the images created in stone by sculptors working in Ireland over a thousand years ago.